COOKBOOK

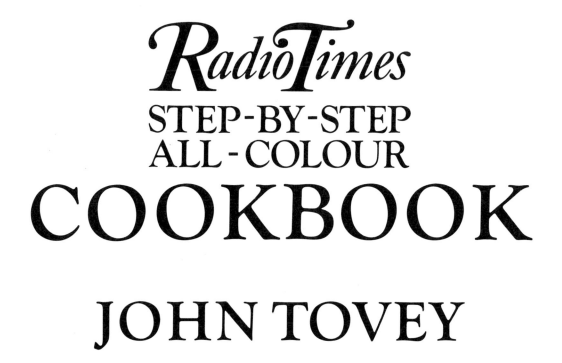

RadioTimes
STEP-BY-STEP
ALL-COLOUR
COOKBOOK

JOHN TOVEY

BBC BOOKS

Published by BBC Books,
a division of BBC Enterprises Limited,
Woodlands, 80 Wood Lane, London W12 0TT

First published 1990
© John Tovey 1990

Reprinted 1990
ISBN 0 563 36028 3
Edited by Sue Fleming
Monitoring editor: Susan Martineau
Designed by Sara Amit
Photographs by Tim Imrie
Food testing and styling by Margaret Armstrong
Printed in England by Clays Ltd, St Ives plc
Colour separation by Technik Ltd, Berkhamsted
Jacket printed by Belmont Press, Northampton

CONTENTS

INTRODUCTION

I HAVE THOROUGHLY enjoyed writing the weekly food column in the *Radio Times* for these last two years, mainly because of the feedback from the letters that arrive weekly via the editor. Most have been nice, friendly and encouraging; though some, I must admit, have been nigh vitriolic in their condemnation of my liking for cream, eggs, sugar, fat, booze and the other good things in life.

Only one recipe provided me with an above-average amount of critical letters, and that was the one for the coffee cake on p. 156. I had deliberately set out to capture the taste of a fabulous bitter gâteau I had once eaten in Austria, but it wasn't appreciated, and the recipe in this book has been duly amended! What caused constant consternation, though, was the apparent contradictions between Dr Barry Lynch's copy (on health) and mine. He outlines all the things that are bad for us; I seem to use every one of them in my cooking, hence all those letters. (However, most of my recipes are for one-off occasions, and eating things that aren't exactly healthy for us can't do too much harm every now and again!) One week Dr Lynch's page loudly proclaimed: 'Food, Poisonous Food', and went on to say how appalling, disgusting, dirty and bad domestic pets were around the house. On the next page I said: 'These evenings are equally relished by my Old English sheepdog . . . who gets to lick up all the leftovers in the pans.' The local postman had to deliver sacks of mail by van from several hundred folk who were infuriated by my having a dog, albeit in my own *home* kitchen. I just put a letter into the word processor and simply said I felt sad that they could not share my joy of animals, as animals have always been part of my domestic scene.

There have been many sincere requests asking different questions about personal culinary problems readers had, and all have been painstakingly answered. With the 'nice' folk I feel I have extended my circle of food friends (those that were less nice got back, after much thought and deliberation, just as much flak as they had flung!), and I hope I was able to help everyone with their problems.

Equipment in the Kitchen

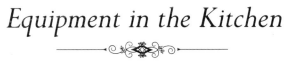

MOST OF THE LETTERS I had from readers concerned equipment. For months, when writing the weekly epistles with carefree abandon, I would mention actual trade names and it took me ages to realize that the subs, armed with enormous blue pencils, immediately struck these out as it isn't done for the *Radio Times* to be seen advertising in any shape or form. Consequently, we tried to get round this by showing as many relevant shots as possible in the small photographs using particular models of marvellous halogen hobs and splendid small electric hand beaters!

Holding my hand firmly on my heart, I must say that I have *not one* commercial string attached to me, but there are several items of kitchenware which I find of infinite use because they are so *practical*. Perhaps to describe what I have and use myself in my own kitchens would be helpful.

First of all, though, a kitchen can have too much clutter – mostly acquired when, like me, you fail to resist going into a new kitchen shop. There, invariably, you discover a new toy which is eagerly taken back home, unpacked, used once, then relegated to the drawer of odds and ends (too fiddly to use, not worth the effort, or just plain useless)!

At my home in Bowness, my whole kitchen work surface is made from local Kirkstone slate, and this has stood up to my messy cooking for 14 years now, and is just as good today as it was when first installed. At the farm I have dark brown Formica which I find more than adequate, but there I also use the new pressed rubber chopping boards as well as old and faithful wooden ones. I would not be without a good food mixer with all the attachments (personally I use a Kenwood). Halogen hobs are for me as I love their instant heat/cool system, and I swear by my fan oven which roasts beautifully. The smaller top oven is marvellous for all types of baking. I also have a microwave now, and am slowly (oh, so slowly) beginning to master the complicated techniques of this type of cooking – mainly rushed dinners for Ozzie, my dog, I must admit. I still have to be convinced that taste does not deteriorate when many recipes are cooked in these contraptions, although I agree they're marvellous for re-heating gravies, sauces and purées when entertaining. And, I must confess, I've discovered that fish steaks are delicious when cooked in the microwave, provided extra herbs are used.

Non-stick baking tins, frying-pans, trays and saucepans are a positive must for me as I am constantly burning things. They are so much easier to clean, although I still have to find one that *never* sticks (despite what they assure you in the sales jargon)! Other necessities are Swiss stainless-steel knives, long-handled spoons, long palette knives, lovely, large, round-bottomed plastic mixing bowls, a six- and a two-slice electric toaster, and an electric coffee filter machine plus a cafetière. I seem to have endless teapots, and thank heavens for jugs with very good V-shaped pouring lips – not the sort that put most of the mix into your receptacle and then spill the balance down the side. I love wooden spoons sought out from old junk shops as they are round-ended, and can get into every 'corner' of the saucepans. Other things that I couldn't live without are metal and plastic strainers, a strong soup ladle, rubber spatulas that are securely attached to their steel handle (the wooden-handled ones shrink with constant use and you find the rubber 'blade' flopping off into your mix), several cooling racks or trays, an oven thermometer that will actually go inside the oven and tell you the *true* temperature, several timing clocks (one that I can actually wear pinned on to my apron!), old-fashioned balancing scales, and large wall-mounted rolls of tinfoil, cling film and kitchen paper. I've also got a plastic salad whizzer-dryer, two stainless-steel ordinary steamers, an electric deep-fryer for all the things one shouldn't eat, a small electric juice extractor which makes light of the early-morning fresh oranges, and a *commercial* waste disposer (for the dishes that don't work when one is test-cooking!).

Ideally, a kitchen should have an endless supply of lovely hot water, a dishwasher, freezer and fridge under the main work surfaces, and lots and lots of three-point electric sockets, all over the place. At the farm I've got a brilliant centre turntable that has numerous compartments to take the tools of my trade. There's a general, very much lived-in feel to the kitchen, with masses of china, glasses, *objets d'art* on the dresser, pictures on the walls and always several huge arrangements of flowers. I also have a couple of speakers wired from my hi-fi, which, in the odd moment of despair, I have on full blast! I mustn't forget the built-in wine racks – and it goes without saying that there's an ever-open bottle 'ready for cooking' in the small fridge.

All this is very important because, for me, the kitchen has to be the hub of the house, where friends and guests feel free and easy to sit, stand, watch, help, fetch, carry and, most important of all, *relax* and *enjoy*. Considering how much time cooks spend in their kitchens, these places should not, in my opinion, be solely work-oriented and clinical!

Entertaining at Home

FOR ME, there is no doubt whatsoever that cooking does give one tremendous satisfaction – there is such joy in breaking bread and taking wine with friends! But it only works properly if *you*, the host or hostess, are *relaxed*. This is why most of the dishes in this book can be prepared ahead of time, which is always such a boon when entertaining. Many dishes can be prepared actually quite far in advance, and frozen – but do remember that they'll need time to come round or defrost. Never try, either, to have three hot courses, for instance. It's not necessary, and causes too much hassle. Serve at least one course cold. When having folk round in the evening, I often make up these cold platters, cover them with cling film and leave them somewhere cool until I need to serve them. Thus *no* last-minute hassle. And *never, ever* do a completely new dish when you have folk coming round. This is a sure recipe for disaster. Use a tried and tested one that you have confidence in.

Put as much thought into the production of the total meal (however simple or grand it may be) from nibbles prior to sitting down, to viewing the state of the kitchen when the guests have departed. When planning your menu, constantly imagine yourself actually in the kitchen getting it together immediately prior to serving. Will you be able to cope without getting your knickers in a twist? Here, I find that course-by-course stacking of the dishwasher a boon, and switching on with Economy 7 makes short and relatively inexpensive work of this task!

As far as china is concerned, it is nice to have one full and completely 'chip-less' dinner service to show off, but I personally tend to seek out part-dinner, fish and dessert services from junk-type shops rather than upmarket antique shops. I couldn't care less if, after I have served a five-course meal, using a different china for each course, a guest goes home and says, 'He's had fun buying up cheap job lots!' In fact, I take it as a compliment, as I have used my *nous* to knock a few bob off the real stuff. I must admit that I do find some of the current 'bargain reject shops' a bit of a rip-off, but anybody travelling through the Potteries should always spare the time and take the trouble to visit the pottery shops there, where seconds can be had at an enormous saving. (Often it is damned nigh impossible to see the fault!)

For the actual table setting, I like to use individual place mats, preferring these to tablecloths. I am fortunate enough to be able to buy these mats on our annual working trip to the States each early March when Bloomingdales seem to have their 'white' sale. I come back armed with them, and napkins to match. If you are a dab hand at the sewing machine, though, it is often possible to make up some place settings and matching napkins from roll ends of material from your local market.

Fresh flowers are a must when entertaining, but I rarely have them on the actual table. I have masses in the room where we are going to dine, though, and elsewhere in the house. I always take the flowers *out* of the dining room after the guests have gone, and leave them in the cool of the garage. Somehow, either the heat given off by the guests or the vibrant noise seems to affect them. They last much longer if given this rest from my brand of entertaining!

Other things to put your mind to for an entertaining evening are lighting (candles are particularly complementary to setting and guests), background music (at the right sort of volume to overcome a sudden lull in conversation), a coffee tray discreetly laid with everything ready for the end of the meal, and a little 'take-away' home-cooked goodie for departing guests. Most important of all, though, is either a spare bottle of your favourite wine or a vacuum flask of the hot toddy on p. 173 secretly kept to hand. These are *yours* for the final treat of the evening, when you at last sit down, relax and mull over how the occasion went.

I do hope that the recipes and ideas in this book will help turn all such entertaining occasions into huge successes!

Apple and mushroom soup

I MAKE APOLOGIES to my Miller Howe customers and readers of my cookery books for making them suffer yet again the secrets of super soups. But once you have mastered this basic recipe, you can ring the changes in so many ways (using the basic 2 lb/900 g vegetables). For there is nothing more satisfying for a simple supper than a huge bowl of home-made cream of vegetable soup with lovely hot bread from the oven covered with lashings of delicious butter. In my childhood this was the dish of the day on Thursday, when funds were low.

Soups are easy to make, simple to serve, a joy to devour — and relatively easy on the pocket. I make no bones (no pun meant for vegetarians!) about the fact that home-made stock is essential: it definitely makes all the difference to the end product. One of my favourite weekly dishes at the farm is roast local chicken (my Old English sheepdog shares this view). There is practically no meat at all left on the chicken carcass when it is popped into a large, deep, thick-bottomed saucepan to start off the stock. A few days before you need the stock, start collecting the following in a large plastic bag in the salad drawer of your fridge: outer leaves and base stalks of lettuce, fairly clean peelings from most root vegetables (not potatoes), skins of garlic cloves — in fact, many items which you are about to throw away should be saved and stored for the stockpot. An onion, carrot, bay leaf and parsley can be added.

Put all these on and around the chicken carcass in a large pan and cover with cold water. Set over a medium heat and bring to simmering point. Reduce the heat and simmer slowly for as long as possible (I sometimes keep it going for 36 hours), constantly checking to ensure it isn't boiling, and replenishing the ingredients, particularly the cold water. When your stock is ready (photo 1), pass it through a sieve.

1 Use flavourful vegetables and trimmings with cold water and a chicken carcass to make a soup stock.

2 Cover the vegetable mixture with doubled and dampened greaseproof paper before simmering the soup.

3 To ensure smoothness, and remove any stalks, pips or skin, sieve the soup after liquidising.

Serves 6–12, depending on size of bowl

4 oz (100 g) butter, cut into pieces

8 oz (225 g) onions, peeled and finely chopped (see p.31)

1 lb (450 g) apples

1 lb (450 g) mushrooms, cleaned

5 fl oz (150 ml) inexpensive sherry

1½ pints (900 ml) home-made stock

salt or sugar

Garnish

whipping cream

fresh herbs

Over a low heat, melt the butter in a large saucepan. Add the prepared onions, and cook slowly for about 10 minutes, until golden. Meanwhile wipe the apples with a damp cloth and simply cut each into eight sections through the core (do not discard the core, or peel the apples). Add to the cooked onions along with the cleaned mushrooms.

Put in the sherry and stir together until the ingredients are well mixed. Cover with a double thickness of damp greaseproof paper of sufficient size to come up the sides of the pan a little way (photo 2). Cover with a lid and simmer for 40–45 minutes, looking in from time to time to ensure that the mixture is not dry.

The apples are fairly soft after this cooking time, and the ingredients look very unappetising! Add the strained stock. Half-fill a liquidiser with this mixture – ensuring that you do not have all stock and no body, or vice versa – and liquidise until it is quite runny.

If you do not have a liquidiser, beat all the ingredients together in a saucepan with an electric whisk.

Whichever you use, always pass the mixture through a coarse sieve into a large bowl to make sure that there are no pieces of stalk or skin to play merry hell with somebody's dentures! (This is easily done using a large metal sieve and a metal soup ladle, photo 3.)

When required, re-heat slowly over a low heat and always then check the seasoning – if too sweet add salt, if salty add sugar. Garnish each bowl with cream and herbs.

AND TO DRINK

With the apple and mushroom soup (or, for that matter, with any cream of vegetable soup) a glass of your favourite sherry is a must. However, for something different, try a Madeira or, as I do occasionally, a glass of Marsala that has been extremely well chilled.

Chilled soup

WHEN I FIRST OPENED *Miller Howe in July 1971, the weather was tropical and neither the small dining room nor the kitchen was air-conditioned. I resorted to serving chilled soups in order to save one more gas hob and to do without a warming cupboard for the bowls.*

They were met with either acclaim or discord. Why, oh why, when a guest starts to make a disparaging remark in a theatrical stage whisper, does the restaurant always happen to be silent? I clearly remember serving the apricot and hazelnut soup for the first time. A regular North Country couple had the diners in hoots of laughter at the end of the soup course. When taking in the last spoonful, the husband said to his wife, 'Alice, this soup's not too hot — how's yours?' 'Likewise,' was the reply. 'Shall we send it back?' 'Nay, I've finished mine. But I can't say I liked it much!'

Many conventionally made soups (see the preceding recipe) are delicious served chilled — in particular tomato, apple and celery (10 oz/275 g of each ingredient) or tomato and red pepper (1 lb/450 g of each). All cold soups should obviously be made the day before in order to be well chilled (remember also to make space in the fridge for the soup bowls). The final seasoning adjustment should be made just prior to serving — icing sugar brings out some flavours!

Chilled cucumber soup

THIS FIRST RECIPE *is my favourite. The sultanas in brandy are optional — but delicious!*

Serves 6

2 tablespoons sultanas, soaked in 1 tablespoon cooking brandy for at least 24 hours (optional)

1 English cucumber

10 fl oz (300 ml) single cream

10 fl oz (300 ml) natural yoghurt

2 fresh garlic cloves, crushed with 1 level teaspoon salt

1 tablespoon tarragon vinegar

2 level tablespoons chopped fresh mint

2 hard-boiled eggs, finely chopped or grated

2 teaspoons horseradish cream

salt and freshly ground black pepper

Garnish

6 dessertspoons flaked almonds, toasted

2–3 fresh raspberries per person

Wipe the cucumber and grate by hand on a stainless-steel grater into a large bowl (photo 1), then incorporate all the other ingredients, except for the sultanas. I honestly find that the best way to get the garlic and horseradish cream evenly distributed is to put my well-scrubbed hands into the mixture and rub the ingredients together (photo 2). Cover with cling film and leave in the fridge to chill. Add the sultanas prior to serving and adjust the seasoning. Garnish with the toasted almonds and raspberries.

Chilled apricot and hazelnut soup

Serves 12

1 lb (450 g) dried apricots, soaked in 5 fl oz (150 ml) cooking brandy for 24 hours

6 oz (175 g) onions, peeled and finely diced (see p. 31)

3 oz (75 g) butter

1 pint (600 ml) chicken stock (see p. 10)

15 fl oz (450 ml) natural yoghurt

1 pint (600 ml) cold milk

1 oz (25 g) ground hazelnuts

salt and freshly ground black pepper

a little Frangelico liqueur (optional)

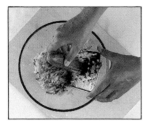

1 For the cucumber soup, grate the wiped cucumber, skin and all, into a large bowl.

2 Mix the ingredients together thoroughly using your hands – don't forget to scrub them well first!

3 For the avocado soup, cut the fruit in half to remove the stone.

4 Scoop the flesh out of the avocado halves using a silver tablespoon.

Garnish

a little natural yoghurt

chopped hazelnuts

Mince the soaked apricots. Fry the onions in the butter, add the minced apricots and then the chicken stock. Simmer for 20 minutes, liquidise and pass through a sieve.

When cold, fold in the yoghurt, milk and ground hazelnuts, and season to taste. If you're feeling extravagant, flavour the soup with some Frangelico liqueur. Top with a little yoghurt and some chopped hazelnuts.

AND TO DRINK

Chilled soups are well accompanied by sherry or Madeira, also chilled.

Chilled avocado, orange and mint soup

Serves 6

4 ripe avocados

juice and finely grated rind of 2 oranges

at least 12 fresh mint leaves

15 fl oz (450 ml) single cream

15 fl oz (450 ml) natural yoghurt

a little cold milk for thinning (optional)

Garnish

orange segments (see p. 15)

sprigs of fresh mint or redcurrants

Prepare the avocados as shown in photos 3 and 4, and place the flesh in a food processor. Bring to a smooth paste with the orange juice and rind, mint and cream. Pass through a plastic sieve into a bowl and fold in the yoghurt. Chill.

This may be too thick for your personal liking – if so, cold milk thins it down admirably. Serve garnished with orange segments and mint, or with a sprig of fresh redcurrants – the latter go well with any of these chilled soups.

Chicken and liver pâté loaf with fresh orange segments

*T*HIS IS AN OLD FAVOURITE *of mine as it is very easy to make, simple to serve, and invariably thoroughly enjoyed by the diners. Even people who generally quibble at the very thought of eating chicken livers happily tackle this, as it requires only 8 oz (225 g) to a 1 lb (450 g) chicken breast.*

I must admit that, when I plan to serve it to VIP guests at home, some liqueur in the mix certainly does add a bit of 'oomph'. The recipe says the chicken livers and the cubed breast should be marinated overnight – but try to marinate for 2–3 days in the fridge as the final flavour will be even better.

Serves 12–16

10–12 rashers smoked back bacon

1 oz (25 g) butter

2 oz (50 g) onions, peeled and finely diced (see p. 31)

3 fresh garlic cloves, peeled and crushed with 1 teaspoon fine sea salt (see p. 17)

8 oz (225 g) chicken livers, cleaned and marinated overnight in 5 fl oz (150 ml) port mixed with 2 tablespoons olive oil

a little olive oil

1 lb (450 g) breast of chicken, boned, cubed and marinated overnight in 5 fl oz (150 ml) cooking brandy

2 medium eggs

2 tablespoons finely chopped mixed fresh herbs (such as tarragon, marjoram, chives, parsley)

½ teaspoon freshly grated nutmeg

finely grated rind of 2 oranges

generous grinding of black pepper

2 oz (50 g) nibbed almonds, toasted

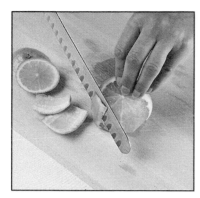

1 For the orange segments, top and tail the fruit with a sharp knife, then cut downwards on a board to remove skin and pith.

2 Over a sieve, with a bowl to catch the juice, cut down into the orange between the flesh and the membrane covering the segments.

3 Cut into the middle of the orange. The membrane-free segments will fall into the sieve.

Garnish

3 oranges, peeled and segmented (photos 1–3)

lettuce or watercress

Melba toast

Pre-heat the oven to gas mark 4, 350°F (180°C). The recipe needs a food processor for swiftness, but if you have only a liquidiser, it can be done in three batches and brought together in a bowl with a beater or whisk.

Line a 2 lb (900 g) non-stick loaf tin with the bacon as illustrated on p. 85, so that the rashers overhang the rim. Leave to one side.

In a frying-pan melt the butter gently and cook the onions and garlic paste until golden. Strain the chicken livers (retaining the booze), add them to the cooked onions and lightly seal. Put this mixture into your food processor with the booze from the livers.

Warm through some oil in the frying-pan and seal off the strained chicken cubes (put the marinade into the food processor). When cooked, add to the other ingredients in the machine.

Add the eggs, herbs, nutmeg, orange rind (always make sure you first wipe the skin with a damp cloth and dry it before grating) and pepper. Turn the machine on and grind until the mixture is a very smooth paste; it will, in fact, be quite runny. It is always wise to stop the machine half-way through blending and, using a spatula, wipe down the sides of the bowl. Fold in the browned nibbed almonds and transfer the mixture to the prepared loaf tin. Knock the mixture down. Flip over the hanging sides of the bacon.

Stand the tin in a bain-marie – a roasting tray half-filled with boiling water – and bake in the pre-heated oven for 45 minutes. Remove from the oven and leave to cool in the tin covered with some tinfoil.

Turn out and slice. Serve on lettuce or watercress with orange segments and Melba toast triangles (toast crustless bread on both sides, cut horizontally in half, then toast briefly again).

AND TO DRINK

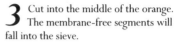

My own taste invariably calls for a wine of the Gewürztraminer type, most obviously from Alsace. However, I'm committed to New World wines, and I suggest the Orlando Eden Valley Gewürztraminer 1986 from Australia or the Matua Valley Gewürztraminer 1987 from New Zealand.

Cheese and herb pâté

I MAKE NO EXCUSES for the fact that cheese and herb pâté is made at least twice a week here at Miller Howe. It is used in endless ways: for stuffing puff pastry cornets, scooped-out cold tomatoes or breasts of chicken; piped with a nozzle into stars and used to garnish cooked baby sweetcorn or grilled fish; or to fill scooped-out red peppers with walnuts down the middle. It can be pressed down into a 1 lb (450 g) loaf tin, chilled and then simply sliced and placed on lettuce, tomato and watercress and a good French-dressed salad. The uses are almost infinite in variety and it's superb for both simple and exotic dishes. It's easy to make, and is always appreciated by guests.

However, a few years ago I received in the post one morning a brown unstamped envelope (on which I had to pay double postage), only to find inside a note addressed simply to 'Tovey' and stating that the writer had made this pâté the week before for some guests who were coming round for dinner. The pâté was atrocious, the guests left early and her husband hadn't spoken to her since. Under the circumstances, could I refund the cost of the ingredients she'd used?

I got the writer's telephone number from directory enquiries and dialled it. I wish I could have seen her face when I said: 'Hello, Mrs So and So. This is John Tovey from Miller Howe. I believe you have problems.'

Ten minutes later, when I had got nowhere, I simply asked if she knew what a clove of garlic was. It transpired that she had used two whole bulbs of garlic to 1 lb of cream cheese instead of two cloves! I mentioned the fact that her husband hadn't spoken to her for a week — with that amount of garlic, I doubt if he could open his mouth!

So a bit of basic information about garlic. Follow photos 1–3, crushing the cloves with salt on a work surface (or a special board kept especially for garlic). Throw away your garlic presses as they are quite useless.

Makes 1¼ lb (550 g)

1 lb (450 g) rich cream cheese

2 fresh garlic cloves, peeled and crushed with 1 teaspoon salt

1 On the left is a whole bulb of garlic, on the right a single clove.

2 Take a small, sharp knife, a peeled garlic clove and some free-running salt, and start chopping the garlic on to the salt.

3 Mash them together until you have an easy-to-use paste.

2 tablespoons chopped fresh herbs (parsley, marjoram, fennel, chives)

4 oz (100 g) butter, melted

In a bowl beat the cream cheese with the crushed garlic and the fresh herbs, and then gently fold the cooled melted butter into the mixture. Do not add the butter while it is hot or the mixture will curdle. Lo and behold, the pâté is ready for use!

Savoury apple with Miller Howe tarragon cream

Serves 6–8

1 egg

2 oz (50 g) caster sugar

2 fl oz (50 ml) tarragon vinegar

10 fl oz (300 ml) double cream

3–4 Granny Smith apples

cheese and herb pâté (see preceding recipe)

Garnish

paprika or redcurrants

sprig of parsley or mint

tiny salads (see method)

In a small pudding bowl (not aluminium) which can be placed comfortably over a pan of simmering water, mix together the egg, sugar and vinegar, and cook – stirring from time to time with a wooden spoon – until the mixture thickens, 10–15 minutes. Leave to cool.

Lightly beat the cream, then strain the cooled egg mixture through a sieve and fold it into the cream.

Meanwhile, but at the last minute, prepare the Granny Smith apples by cutting them in half horizontally – that is, not down through the centre of the core – peeling them, removing the centre core and then cleaning up the stalk and base. Stuff each apple half with some of the cheese and herb pâté, place them flat-side down on a plate and coat liberally with the tarragon cream.

A touch of paprika would add colour and flavour (as would a redcurrant), and then a sprig of parsley, mint or other herb will finish the dish off. You could also serve the apple half with a tiny savoury salad, here a leaf of radicchio, scored orange slice, tomato, spring onion twirl and a radish flower (see p. 111).

AND TO DRINK

I would serve a good strong chilled cider.

Miller Howe utter bliss

*Y*OUR INITIAL REACTION *to the name of this dish could well be that it is simply arrogant to call anything 'utter bliss', but in spite of this I stand by the name. Many of us will have suffered a dinner — perhaps an annual company event — where the starter was chilled melon. An unimposing eighth of a melon pallidly sitting on a bare plate, with perhaps a weeping Maraschino cherry as a garnish — it is often as tough as old boots and invariably* bland. *My recipe is not!*

I can vividly recall the bustling markets of Central Africa where I worked in my earlier days, and how canny the Africans were when it came to buying melons. I know one should discreetly press the base of the fruit to see if it will 'give', normally guaranteeing ripeness; but they used to chatter and argue before pouncing on their spoils, giving the fruit a good sniff and putting it back with scorn if the smell wasn't boozy and sweet. Your greengrocer may not take kindly to this!

I go for the small, round cantaloupe, Charentais, musk and Sponspeck melons, which have a lovely colour and are sweet and pungent. This is, in fact, quite a filling dish and the sparkling wine makes it special. It often suffices for me as a supper dish, provided I have a glass of the wine as an appetiser and can finish the bottle afterwards! This recipe is also excellent for a convalescent who needs cosseting.

Serves 2

1 ripe melon

4 oz (100 g) fresh strawberries or raspberries

1 dessertspoon icing sugar

1 tablespoon cooking brandy (optional)

generous splash of sparkling white wine

sprigs of fresh mint

Wipe the melon with a clean, slightly damp cloth, turn it on its side and cut it through the middle. Nick a little off each end so that the halves will be reasonably stable when placed on the plate.

Using a tablespoon carefully remove the seeds and gungy flesh (photo 1). With a Parisian scoop take out a circle of balls around the rim of the melon, replacing them in the holes round side up (photo 2). At this stage the melon can be covered with cling film and left to chill.

Put the strawberries or raspberries into a liquidiser with the icing sugar and brandy (if using). Purée them and pass through a plastic sieve. If you haven't a liquidiser, they must be painstakingly crushed and then sieved.

For a flash of elegance, when you are ready to assemble the dish, place a doily on each plate together with a small flower and perhaps a fern leaf. Put a chilled, prepared melon half on the plate and carefully dribble the purée around the edge (photo 3): it doesn't matter if some slops into the middle. As you serve, fill the centre of the melon halves with sparkling wine, and finish off with mint sprigs.

Egg flip sauce

A NOTHER WICKED WAY *with chilled melon balls is to put them into a champagne, wine or Manhattan cocktail glass and cover them with a rich egg flip sauce. Photo 4 shows the easy way of making the melon balls, and you can see the finished dish in the main picture.*

Makes nearly 2 pints (1.2 litres)

4 eggs

1 × 14 oz (400 g) tin condensed milk

10 fl oz (300 ml) sherry

5 fl oz (150 ml) cooking brandy

½ fresh nutmeg, finely grated

15 fl oz (450 ml) double cream, whipped

Put all the ingredients except the cream into a bowl and mix them together. Take half of this mixture and blend it little by little with the whipped cream. This should be poured over the melon balls in the glasses.

Serve the balance of the egg flip as an accompanying drink in chilled sherry glasses.

1 Using a tablespoon, carefully remove the seeds and membranes from the melon halves.

2 Scoop out balls from the rim of the melon half and invert them.

3 Dribble the soft fruit purée around the 'holed' rim of the melon.

4 If making a starter from melon balls, use a Parisian scoop and all the flesh of each melon half.

Savoury spiced peach

Serves 4

*E*VER SINCE MY DAYS *in the fifties working in Central Africa as a junior officer, I have had a love of spiced fruit. Tropical fruits were readily available at the local markets, and having gone to Nyasaland from a still-rationed Britain, I was delighted to devour these delicacies. To my mind, nothing compares with those stringy mangoes, enormous sweet peaches, pineapples with a sharp bite that I can still taste today (and the thought of which sends ripples up my spine), and bananas straight from the tree. I soon found myself using them in cooking. Tough meats were made tender by lavish chunks of fruit, and fish from the lake were the better for being baked in banana leaves.*

This snack dish and the one following are both still firm favourites of mine.

The peaches have first to be poached in a spiced stock syrup and you will need, for four peaches, 1 lb (450 g) granulated sugar and 8 fl oz (250 ml) water. Put the sugar and water into a thick-bottomed saucepan and simmer until the sugar dissolves. Add 3 tablespoons white wine vinegar.

Each peach should have four cloves gently pushed into it (one on the top, one on the bottom and one on each side). Poach them gently in the syrup until the skin begins to wrinkle, which means it will come off very easily. Skin the fruit and then leave it in the syrup until quite cold.

Remove the cloves. Using a small, sharp knife cut each peach in two (photo 1) and then slit open using as little pressure as possible (photo 2). The stone can then

be quite easily removed with the aid of a grapefruit knife (photo 3).

The fruit can be reassembled just as it is, but I like to ring the changes. Here are a few ideas for ingredients to spoon into the cavity: wholegrain mustard with ground hazelnuts; cheese and herb pâté (see p. 16); stoned cherries soaked in brandy and coated with ground almonds; shrimps or prawns with mayonnaise; chicken liver pâté. The peach can be coated with curry mayonnaise (see p. 171) and generously sprinkled with toasted desiccated coconut as in the main picture. Spiced peach halves are delicious when served with toasted sandwiches, and make a change from a pineapple ring as a garnish for ham.

1 Carefully cut each cold spiced peach in half.

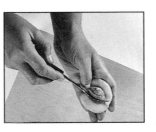

2 Ease the halves apart very carefully.

Baked banana with bacon

For a supper dish (accompanied by a mixed salad) you require 1 banana and 2 rashers of bacon per person. I use smoked middle rashers.

The bananas should be peeled, cut in half through the middle (not lengthways), and then wrapped in bacon (photo 4). Lay on a baking tray and, when you want to cook, simply bake in a pre-heated oven at gas mark 4, 350°F (180°C) for 15 minutes. You can either serve the dish as it is with a simple but effective garnish of some lime slices, salad leaves and radishes (as in the main photo), or you can serve it with curry mayonnaise (see p. 171) and toasted desiccated coconut.

You could also enclose the bacon-wrapped banana in puff pastry (see p. 144) and bake at a higher temperature – gas mark 8, 450°F (230°C) – until puffed and golden, just like a sausage roll!

3 Remove the stone with a grapefruit knife.

4 Simply cut the bananas in half, then wrap in bacon.

AND TO DRINK

A Gewürztraminer would go well with either dish.

Savoury cheese peach on croûton

*T*INNED PEACH HALVES! I can already hear some folk complaining. But why not, I ask? They are firm, full of flavour, and so easy to handle. If you wish to use fresh fruit, there is nothing to stop you — we do use them up at Miller Howe — but they are quite a bind to prepare (see p. 20). Anyway, the strongly flavoured filling gives this dish quite a kick and blends beautifully with the sweet, syrupy, tinned fruit.

As usual when entertaining, the joy of the dish is that all the preparation may be done ahead of time, after which just 10 minutes in the evening and a quick flash under the grill has the dish ready to serve.

When ready to serve, a generous grinding of black pepper will enhance the dish. Also, for my personal taste, I tend to increase the amount of mustard used in the topping, or I beat a little Dijon mustard into the cheese and herb pâté. Some friends who serve this dish regularly are extremely generous with Worcestershire sauce in the grated cheese topping, but if you are serving wine with the dish the sauce does tend to overpower it.

However, the first time you make this, trust the recipe, and when eating it let your own tastebuds dictate any adjustments for the second time around.

Serves 6

6 tinned or fresh peach halves

3 oz (75 g) cheese and herb pâté (see p. 16) or Boursin

Topping

5 oz (150 g) strong Cheddar cheese, grated

1 medium egg, lightly beaten

2 teaspoons cooking brandy (optional)

salt and freshly ground black pepper

1 generous teaspoon Dijon mustard or moutarde de Meaux

To serve

6 × 3 in (7.5 cm) round croûtons (see p. 29 or 30)

6 rashers smoked back bacon, rolled (optional)

Lay the peach halves in your baking dish and either pipe (photo 1) or spoon the cheese and herb pâté or Boursin into the cavities. To make the topping, combine all the ingredients into a paste and divide into six portions. Place these on top of the cheese and herb pâté (photo 2). Place the peaches in a bun tin and cover with cling film until you wish to cook them.

Pre-heat the oven to gas mark 4, 350°F (180°C), when you are ready to cook. Place the croûtons on a small baking tray and, if you're planning to use them as a side garnish, the bacon rolls on another.

The bacon tray should be put in the oven 15 minutes prior to serving time. The prepared peaches take 10 minutes to warm through (photo 3), and the croûtons take only 5 minutes. Photo 4 shows all three ingredients ready for assembling, and the main picture shows the finished dish plus a little garnish salad. The strong iodine flavour of good fresh watercress is an ideal and eye-catching base, painted with a good French dressing.

VARIATIONS

Try a walnut half placed in each peach cavity before the pâté; a generous sprinkling of fresh herbs (rosemary is particularly suitable) scattered over the dish prior to taking to the table; dry English mustard or the merest touch of curry powder added to the cheese topping.

1 Pipe the soft cheese and herb pâté into the cavity of the peach halves.

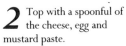

2 Top with a spoonful of the cheese, egg and mustard paste.

3 Place the half peaches in bun tins and warm through in the oven.

4 Ready to serve – warm peaches with croûtons and bacon rolls.

AND TO DRINK

The wine should be a gutsy Gewürztraminer or an Australian Sémillon.

Beef tomatoes

*T*HE COMMON TOMATO *originated in Mexico and South America and did not appear in Europe until the end of the sixteenth century when it was known as the 'love apple'. Nowadays Mediterranean cooking would be lost without it, most commercial kitchens find a daily use for it, and a burger without tomato ketchup would be like fried fish without chips.*

In my early days I was always suspicious of tomatoes, as my father was once rushed to hospital to have his appendix out and swore to his dying day it would not have been necessary if my mother hadn't bombarded him with tomatoes!

In those days the season was short — July to September — but nowadays, with modern refrigeration and transportation methods, tomatoes are available (in varying degrees of texture and flavour, I must admit) all year round. Unfortunately the Dutch and Guernsey growers have a lot to answer for — due to sheer commercial greed. However, the lovely large beef or beefsteak tomatoes that are grown in Morocco, Italy and Provence are delicious. Serve them as a starter, or supper dish.

The herb that should always be used with tomatoes is fresh basil, the ideal partner. This originates from India, where a close relation is apparently sacred and used in religious rites and superstitions. In Provence and Italy one often sees huge tubs of basil growing on restaurant patios as it is supposed to keep flies away! It never seems to keep them away from me — but perhaps they like my aftershave . . .

Beef tomato stuffed with cheese and herb pâté

Serves 2

2 beef tomatoes, skinned (see p. 169)

1/2 teaspoon caster sugar

1/2 teaspoon chopped fresh basil

3 oz (75 g) cheese and herb pâté (see p. 16)

Optional garnish

fresh mint

Lay the skinned tomato stalk-side down and, using a very sharp, small knife, cut in two-thirds of the way down from one side, about ¼ in (5 mm) from the top (photo 1). Gently ease this back and with a Parisian scoop, clean out the tomato (photo 2), putting the gunge into a stockpot. Sprinkle the base and sides with the sugar and chopped basil and then pipe in the cheese and herb pâté in sufficient quantity to keep the lid open at an angle like that of a grand piano (photo 3). Chill and serve, garnished with mint if you like.

Baked sliced tomato on minced mushrooms with cheese

Serves 2

1 oz (25 g) butter

4 oz (100 g) mushrooms, cleaned and minced

2 beef tomatoes, skinned

2 teaspoons chopped fresh basil

4 tablespoons double cream mixed with 1 medium egg, salt and freshly ground black pepper

2 oz (50 g) Cheddar cheese, grated, mixed with 1 oz (25 g) fresh breadcrumbs

Pre-heat the oven to gas mark 4, 350°F (180°C), and rub the butter over the base of an ovenproof dish.

Spread the minced mushrooms on to this, then slice the tomatoes (photo 4) and spread them on top with the basil. Pour over the seasoned cream and egg mix, place in the pre-heated oven and bake for 20 minutes.

Have your grill nice and hot. Scatter the mixed cheese and breadcrumbs on top of the tomato dish and flash under the grill until brown and bubbling.

1 Carefully cut a lid in the skinned tomato – but not quite through, leaving a 'hinge'.

2 Clean the inside of the tomato using a Parisian scoop.

3 Pipe in enough cheese and herb pâté to keep the lid propped open.

4 To slice a beef tomato, hold it steady with a fork and cut through using a very sharp knife.

Garnish

Sprigs of parsley

Pre-heat the oven to gas mark 4, 350°F (180°C).

In each prepared tomato half scatter the caster sugar, mustard and basil. Add the peas and sweetcorn, and place the cheese circle on top. Place on a baking tray and cook in the pre-heated oven for 20 minutes. Garnish with fresh parsley.

VARIATIONS

Buttered eggs (p. 44) are delicious on top of the tomato halves too! Or add a generous sprinkling of grated Cheddar cheese after taking the dish out of the oven, and then brown it under a hot grill.

AND TO DRINK

A glass of chilled sherry or Madeira would be delicious with the savoury tomato half.

Baked savoury beef tomato half

Serves 2

1 beef tomato, skinned and cut in half, seeds and gunge carefully removed

pinch each of caster sugar and dry English mustard

1/2 teaspoon chopped fresh basil

1/2 oz (15 g) each of frozen peas and sweetcorn, defrosted

2 circles Bel Paese cheese, sold in 1 oz (25 g) portions

Savoury onion cups

*L*AST YEAR FRIENDS *and I spent our annual get-together visiting the Italian lakes. Several meals were memorable for their gourmet quality, others for their basic regional fare, but one that stands out in my mind is a lunch we had on the island of Comacina in Lake Como where Benvenuto Puricelli cooks with wonderful flair and panache.*

As we sat down on the terrace, and before we had time to take in the spectacular views or even think about food, a bottle of Frascati was put on the table, followed by hand-painted bowl after bowl containing plain cold vegetables, among them fennel, carrots, chicory, tomatoes, artichokes and peppers. The one that caught our eye, though, contained enormous half onions seemingly baked in their skins.

In their skins they had *been baked, after having been sprinkled generously with coarsely ground coriander seeds and having had lots of rich olive oil poured over them. We devoured the lot, and had the temerity to ask for more. As I stuffed my face yet again, I thought of how I could sophisticate the dish for a first course at Miller Howe. The following recipe is the result, using an old favourite of mine, mushroom pâté.*

Makes 6 onion cups

1 large onion, with thick skin

4 tablespoons olive oil

1 heaped teaspoon coarsely ground coriander seeds

salt and freshly ground black pepper

1 small egg

6 level tablespoons ground hazelnuts

6 tablespoons mushroom pâté (see following recipe)

Topping

5 fl oz (150 ml) double cream

1 large egg

2 teaspoons grated Parmesan cheese

Garnish

sprigs of fresh dill or fennel

1 Sprinkle the onion halves with olive oil and coriander before baking.

2 Remove the centres from the cooked onion halves and use six of the largest 'cups'.

3 Smooth in the egg and hazelnut paste to plug the hole in each cup.

4 Divide the topping between the filled onion cups before baking finally.

Pre-heat the oven to gas mark 6, 400°F (200°C).

Cut the onion in half through its 'equator', and tuck both halves into a snug container. Pour on the oil and sprinkle with the coriander (photo 1). Bake in the pre-heated oven for 1½ hours. Remove and allow to go cold.

Lift out the centres of the onion halves (use these in onion purées or soups) and take the three largest remaining 'cups' from each half (photo 2), so that you have six cups in all. Place on a greased baking tray and lightly season them.

Make a paste of the small egg and the hazelnuts, and smooth into the bottom of the six cups (photo 3). This plugs the holes in the base of the onion cups. On each hazelnut base spread 1 tablespoon of mushroom pâté, cover with cling film and put in the fridge to get really cold.

When ready to cook, pre-heat the oven to gas mark 4, 350°F (180°C). Mix together the topping ingredients and divide between the onion cups (in photo 4, I am using just four cups). Bake in the pre-heated oven for 15 minutes and serve garnished with fresh dill or fennel sprigs. I have served the onion cups shown in the main picture with a simple spinach and nutmeg purée, and tomato sauce (see p. 35).

Mushroom pâté

This pâté has endless uses, and can be frozen in small containers as a marvellous stand-by.

Makes about 14 oz (400 g)

2 oz (50 g) butter

4 oz (100 g) onions, peeled and minced

1 lb (450 g) mushrooms, cleaned and minced (stalks and skins included)

10 fl oz (300 ml) red wine

Simply melt the butter in a saucepan and add the other ingredients. Stir them together well. Simmer over a medium heat until the sloppy mush becomes fairly dry and firm – about 1 hour.

AND TO DRINK

A robust Cabernet Sauvignon from Chile would go well!

Baked red pepper with tomato

PEPPERS ONLY STARTED to become popular in this country in the early fifties and then just for a limited summer period. They were astronomically expensive and quite a talking point. Wild varieties had always been eaten in South America, but it wasn't until Christopher Columbus discovered them in the New World that they became known in Europe. They featured substantially in Mediterranean cooking, but it was Elizabeth David who was primarily responsible for making them popular in Great Britain through her books, from her first, Mediterranean Food, *in 1950, through to her fifth in 1960,* French Provincial Cooking. *In fact many of us 'foodies' in this day and age owe an enormous amount to this truly remarkable lady. All her paperbacks are on the cookery shelves here at Miller Howe, and all are dishevelled, well thumbed and rather faded and jaded in looks. They still inspire, though!*

Nowadays peppers are on greengrocery and supermarket shelves throughout the year, and the basic red or green are now supplemented by yellow, white and purple ones (heaven forbid)! The green I find gives me awful indigestion, the yellow does nothing for me, but oh, the red, the red! It is sweet, succulent, tempting, delicious and versatile: it can transform a soup or a sauce; make the base for the perfect supper platter; and blow your mind if made into a pickle or marmalade! I am told that it helps stomach and kidney ailments and counteracts flatulence. This might be true if the pepper were simply eaten by itself, but, as usual, all the garlic, oil, etc., I put with it soon chases all these old wives' tales out of the window!

Many cookery writers insist that you remove the skins of peppers, but this, for me, is a very tedious task and, I think, removes a great deal of the actual flavour and fibre content. When buying, always look for bright shiny skins and never, ever, buy a pepper that is slightly wrinkled as, like us, that reveals its age! Store in the salad drawer of the fridge.

Simon Hopkinson is the head chef at the ever-popular Bibendum restaurant in London, which I frequent as often as possible (the lunch menu is a bargain). He, too, is an ardent fan of Elizabeth David. It is his Piedmont pepper dish that I emulate here, and which is now very popular in the Miller Howe repertoire.

Serves 2 as a starter or 1 as a main course

1 red pepper

2 fat, juicy garlic cloves, peeled

2 teaspoons chopped fresh parsley or basil (when available)

2 tomatoes, skinned (see p. 169)

2 teaspoons walnut oil (optional)

4 tablespoons good-quality olive oil

salt and freshly ground black pepper

Croûtons

1 large slice thin white bread

1 tablespoon olive oil plus 1 knob of butter, melted together

Topping

4 tinned anchovy fillets (optional)

generous sprinkling of freshly grated Parmesan or strong Cheddar cheese

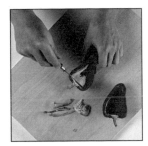

1 Remove the white pith and seeds from the pepper halves with a small, sharp knife, leaving stalks on.

2 Squash the garlic sliver on a work surface (or board) with a palette knife to let the juice run freely.

3 Place the skinned tomatoes on top of the garlic in the pepper halves.

4 The baked pepper halves *should* look a little black at the edges.

Pre-heat the oven to gas mark 6, 400°F (200°C).

Wipe the pepper with a clean, damp cloth and cut in half lengthways. With a small, sharp, pointed knife remove any white pith and seeds (photo 1), but leave the stalk intact on the end.

Cut the garlic cloves into three or four strips, lay these on your work surface and, using a palette knife, flatten and squash them to let the juice run freely (photo 2). Place these strips on the base of your prepared red pepper halves, then sprinkle on the chopped parsley or basil. Put the whole skinned tomatoes on top (photo 3). Pour 1 teaspoon of the walnut oil (if using) into the base of each pepper half, and then transfer to your cooking dish (preferably one that will just take the peppers comfortably, so that they don't flop or fall apart). Pour 2 tablespoons of the olive oil over each pepper half and season with salt and pepper. Bake in the pre-heated oven for at least 1½ hours. The pepper halves should now look slightly black and burned round the edges (photo 4).

About 20 minutes before the end of the cooking time, remove the crust from the bread slice, cut into two rectangles (or better still, with a cutter, into two ovals) and dip in the heated olive oil and butter mixture, allowing it all to be soaked up. Lay the bread shapes on a baking tray and cook for 10–15 minutes in the oven alongside the peppers. Remove and put on a double thickness of kitchen paper to drain.

When you wish to serve, simply transfer the pepper halves to the bread croûtons, put two anchovy fillets diagonally over each tomato and coat with grated cheese. I strongly suspect that even the most timid of guests could take two halves as a starter!

Do not throw out any oil left in the pepper dish, but keep in a screw-top jar as it will have developed an interesting sweet pepper flavour. (You could use it in something like the fried monkfish cubes on p. 62.)

AND TO DRINK

This is a tricky one. I think a robust red Rhône would be able to stand up to all those strong, delicious flavours.

Mushroom pyramid on peanut butter croûton

*T*HE JOY OF THIS RECIPE *and the one following is that practically everything can be done ahead of serving time, allowing you to mix with your guests. Ready-sliced bread is ideal for the croûtons. Use any fresh chopped garden herb as a garnish.*

Serves 6

6 thin slices of bread

4 tablespoons olive or other oil

2 oz (50 g) butter

1 lb (450 g) small mushroom caps, peeled

at least 12 oz (350 g) peanut butter (smooth or crunchy)

Garnish

sprigs of fresh herbs

With a 3 in (7.5 cm) round, fluted cutter, cut a croûton from each slice of bread. In a frying-pan gently heat half the oil and then add to this the butter broken up in to teaspoon-sized pieces. Cook the croûtons in this until brown and crisp, turning from time to time. Then transfer to a tray covered with a double thickness of kitchen paper so that they can drain dry. Leave to cool.

Meanwhile, add the remaining oil to the pan and cook the mushroom caps for about 5 minutes. Drain these as well on kitchen paper and leave to cool.

Spread each croûton generously with peanut butter and put 2 tablespoons of peanut butter in the middle of each to form a pyramid. Build the mushroom caps up around the peanut butter.

When you wish to serve, pre-heat the oven to gas mark 4, 350°F (180°C). Place the mushroom pyramids in the pre-heated oven for 10 minutes.

Devilled mushrooms

A LOT OF RECIPES, including this one, call for finely diced onions, but so many cooks find them difficult to prepare. Some find themselves seeking plasters after cutting themselves as well as the onions! In fact, they are relatively easy to prepare as you will see from the step-by-step photographs.

Serves 6

1 tablespoon olive oil

1 oz (25 g) butter

8 oz (225 g) small mushroom caps, peeled

3 oz (75 g) onions, peeled and finely diced

finely grated rind of 1 lemon

1 tablespoon lemon juice

10 fl oz (300 ml) double cream

1 teaspoon white wine vinegar

1 tablespoon bottled tomato sauce

1 teaspoon Worcestershire sauce

½ teaspoon dry English mustard

1 teaspoon soft brown sugar

1 teaspoon soy sauce

salt and freshly ground black pepper

Garnish

6 sprigs of parsley or watercress

1 To chop an onion, lay each peeled half in turn flat on the work surface and, using a small, sharp knife, cut several times three-quarters of the way through from the stalk to the root.

2 Gripping the onion firmly, cut down vertically through the horizontal cuts.

3 Cut through the other way, allowing the onion dice to fall free.

In a frying-pan over a medium heat slowly heat the olive oil and add the butter. When melted and combined, seal the mushroom caps, then transfer them to a tray lined with kitchen paper to drain. Cook the finely diced onions in the same pan until soft and drain also.

Divide the mushrooms and onion between six small ovenproof dishes, cover with cling film and leave them until needed. Meanwhile, mix all the other ingredients together in a small saucepan and put to one side.

When ready to cook, pre-heat the oven to gas mark 4, 350°F (180°C). Heat through the dishes of mushrooms and onion in the oven, standing them in a roasting tray partly filled with warm water for 10 minutes. At the same time heat the ingredients in the saucepan and, just before serving, pour this hot sauce over the mushrooms and onions and garnish with a sprig of parsley or watercress.

AND TO DRINK

With both of these mushroom recipes, I would drink a chilled Beaujolais.

Aubergine loaf

*A*UBERGINE IS ACTUALLY the French name for this plant — in English it is the eggplant. When buying, look for one which is tight and shiny because, as with humans, a wrinkly skin betokens age! If you are not using it immediately, it is best stored in the salad compartment of the fridge.

Aubergines are always eaten cooked — moussaka and ratatouille are just two favourite dishes of mine. In Lebanon there is a delicious dip known as poor man's caviar, and in Turkey there's Imam bayildi (which means 'the Imam fainted' — from pleasure!). Aubergine circles dipped in batter and deep-fried are also superb, but here I explain how to make an aubergine loaf which can be served hot, warm or cold.

The loaf can be sliced thickly and served by itself, or on sliced tomatoes with grated cheese on top, or with yoghurt which has a little wholegrain mustard mixed into it, or topped with fried tomatoes with lots of garlic, or used as a base for scrambled or poached eggs, or topped with mashed banana, preserved ginger and more nuts — but I like it in the following way, with an apple slice topped with peanut butter. Take a Granny Smith apple, wipe it with a damp cloth and remove the core (photo 1). Put the apple on its side, cut into thin slices (photo 2) and either pipe or spoon peanut butter on to the slices. Sprinkle circles of spring onion over the lot.

Serves 8–12

1 lb (450 g) aubergines
salt
butter for greasing
4 medium eggs
4 oz (100 g) stale breadcrumbs
3 oz (75 g) Parmesan cheese, grated
2 tablespoons chopped fresh basil
5 fl oz (150 ml) olive oil
3 fat, juicy garlic cloves, peeled
2 tablespoons tomato purée

1 tablespoon Worcestershire sauce

2 tablespoons chopped fresh parsley

freshly ground black pepper

3 oz (75 g) nibbed almonds or walnuts, macadamia, hazel or pecan nuts, finely chopped

Wipe the aubergines with a damp cloth and cut in half lengthways. Place skin-side down on a cooling rack over a double thickness of kitchen paper. Sprinkle liberally with free-running salt (photo 3) and leave lightly covered with cling film for 2–3 hours. The aubergines will sweat and drip on to the kitchen paper.

Pre-heat the oven to gas mark 6, 400°F (200°C). Lightly grease a 2 lb (900 g) loaf tin with butter.

Place all the ingredients except the aubergines and almonds (or other nuts) in a food processor and whisk together until smooth. Meanwhile, pat the aubergines dry and mince or chop fairly finely. Spread the almonds or other chopped nuts on a baking tray and cook gently in the pre-heating oven until they begin to brown.

Incorporate the aubergines and nuts into the mixture and pour it into your prepared tin (photo 4). Put the tin in the pre-heated oven and cook for 20 minutes, then turn the oven down to gas mark 4, 350°F (180°C). Cook for a further 20 minutes. Open the oven door and test that the mix is cooked by putting a skewer gently into the middle – it should come out clean. If it is still slightly soggy, return it to the oven and cook for a further 5–10 minutes.

When the loaf is cooked, remove it from the oven and leave for 10 minutes covered with tinfoil or a tea towel. It is then ready to turn out.

1 A favourite accompaniment is a Granny Smith apple, cored with a corer.

2 Slice the cored apple, and top each slice with peanut butter.

3 Place the aubergines on a cooling rack over kitchen paper and sprinkle flesh liberally with free-running salt.

4 Combine all the ingredients for the loaf and pour into a greased loaf tin.

AND TO DRINK

Try a New World Merlot.

Vegetable terrine

SHOULD YOU THINK vegetable terrine is beyond your capabilities, let me categorically say, here and now, that it isn't! Fiddly and time-consuming, yes, but when your guests and you sit down to eat it, just think – some restaurants charge £6.95 for a slice of this masterpiece. I doubt if your whole finished dish costs as much!

There is little new in cooking, but I do remember that this particular dish was part of the original nouvelle cuisine craze, when it was made with mild ham, egg whites, lemon and special oil. It all had to be done very quickly so that the 'paste mixture' wouldn't fall. Needless to say, there is no fear of this happening if you follow this recipe; the chicken breast, eggs and cream make the basic binding.

Anyway, certain dishes do deserve time and care, and this is one. Most professional establishments use commercial steel terrine moulds for this, but as they are terribly expensive I have adapted the Miller Howe recipe to be cooked in a 2 lb (900 g) non-stick loaf tin, which obviously gives you a larger individual slice. If you haven't got a 900 g tin, use two 1 lb (450 g) tins. In this case your slices will be smaller, so you will either cut the end product thicker or give each guest two slices!

Serves 8–12

1 lb (450 g) chicken breasts, without bone or skin
salt and freshly ground black pepper
4 egg whites
10 fl oz (300 ml) double cream
butter for greasing

Vegetables

5 outside leaves of a large iceberg lettuce
2 oz (50 g) white of leeks
3 oz (75 g) red peppers
2 oz (50 g) carrots
2 oz (50 g) thin French beans
4 oz (100 g) whole baby sweetcorn

The night before you want to serve the dish, cut the raw chicken breasts into cubes. Place in your food processor with the salt and pepper and blend until fairly smooth, adding the egg whites one at a time. Leave to chill in the fridge for at least 12 hours.

In the meantime, prepare the vegetables. Blanch the lettuce leaves briefly in boiling salted water, drain and cool. Cut the leeks, peppers and carrots into strips roughly the same length and thickness as the French beans (see p. 95 for instructions); leave the baby sweetcorn whole. Blanch all these in boiling salted water, refresh in cold. Pat dry on kitchen paper.

Return the overnight chicken mix to the food processor and, on high speed, slowly dribble in the double cream. Divide the mixture into six portions. Lightly butter and season a 2 lb (900 g) loaf tin and line with the blanched lettuce leaves, making sure that the stem end is on the tin's base (photo 1).

Gently spread one-sixth of the chicken mix on the bottom of the tin using a spatula, and then push the prepared French beans into this (photo 2). Cover the beans with a further layer of the chicken mix (photo 3) and continue, layer by layer, with vegetable strips and chicken mix, until you have used up all the vegetables (follow the main picture if you like). Finish with a layer of chicken mix and flap over the lettuce to cover the top (photo 4). Cover with doubled tinfoil.

Pre-heat the oven to gas mark 4, 350°F (180°C). Place the loaf tin in a roasting tray and pour 1 in (2.5 cm) of hot water around it. Bake in the oven for 40 minutes, then remove, leave to get cold, and chill slightly in the fridge. Turn out the terrine and slice.

Tomato and basil sauce

*C*OLD, THIS GOES NICELY *with the vegetable terrine. It can also be served hot.*

2 tablespoons olive oil

1 oz (25 g) softened butter

2–4 garlic cloves, peeled and crushed

6 oz (175 g) onions, peeled and finely chopped

2 lb (900 g) tomatoes (preferably beef), quartered

5 fl oz (150 ml) cooking sherry or chicken stock

salt and freshly ground black pepper

2 tablespoons soft brown sugar

2 tablespoons chopped fresh basil (or more, according to taste)

Heat the oil and butter in a saucepan, add the crushed garlic and chopped onions, and cook for 10 minutes. Add the quartered tomatoes and all the other ingredients. Cook slowly, uncovered, for 30–45 minutes. Pass through a coarse sieve.

1 Line the greased loaf tin with the blanched lettuce leaves, stalk ends to the base, leaving some overhanging.

2 Start with a layer of chicken mix, then push in the prepared beans.

3 Cover the beans with more chicken mix, building up the layers of vegetable and chicken.

4 Finish with a chicken layer, then bring back the overhanging leaves to cover the terrine completely.

AND TO DRINK

To accompany this dish I recommend a well-chilled Chardonnay.

Avocado savoury cups

*I*F YOU EVER *get sunburned, mashed avocado rubbed over the area is a marvellous soother; I can recommend this from personal experience as, in the Zimbabwe bush recently, I ran out of the normal suntan creams and avocado came to my rescue! However, it is much more commonly used in cooking these days, particularly as it is now cultivated in several countries.*

The avocado became known to Europeans as early as 1519 when a Spanish explorer found the tree on the mainland of Colombia. Wild avocados vary in size, and a few years ago over a period of four weeks I watched one particular fruit enlarge by the day in a Cape Town garden. It became a daily act of awe to inspect it, and in the end my hostess gently swathed it in mosquito net which was tied securely to the branch above. When it was eventually picked, it weighed just over 2 lb (900 g), but needed a lot of jiggery pokery to render it palatable as a soup!

The skin colour of avocados can be confusing as it ranges from acid green, through butter yellow to a wrinkled purple, all according to type. The flesh, when ripe, is a soft lime colour with a buttery texture and taste. I use avocados in a variety of ways. They are extremely versatile in soups, mousses, mayonnaise or cream sauce, and particularly useful in starters, as this recipe shows. You can make one fruit go a long way if you cut it into thin wedges and use similar-sized fresh pear wedges alongside, as well as fresh orange segments. Another good combination is avocado balls with prawns, diced red peppers, chopped apple marinated in fresh lime juice, and toasted cashew nuts, topped with a spoonful of natural yoghurt. Here, I serve avocado in pastry 'cups'.

The best pastry for these cups is the lightly curried one on p. 40. The joy of this dish is that everything is prepared ahead of time and then simply brought together just prior to serving. It looks good, and the combination of flavours is always favourably commented on.

Serve one filled cup per person as a starter. Because it's all so simple, I haven't spelled out quantities in any detailed sense.

To make the cups, prepare and roll out the pastry as described on p. 147, then cut into rounds to fit your bun tins. Shape handles from the rolled pastry left over. These aren't essential, by the way, but make a talking-point. Chill the pastry while you pre-heat the oven to gas mark 3, 325°F (160°C). Bake the pastry cups and handles blind in the oven until golden; watch that the handles don't become *too* brown. Remove from the oven and leave to cool.

When ready to serve, put a blob of home-made mayonnaise (see p. 166) in the base of each cup (photo 1), and then on top of this 1 teaspoon skinned, seeded and chopped tomato (photo 2). Place around this small wedges of avocado that have been prepared ahead of time and lightly coated with fresh lemon juice to prevent discoloration. Follow this with very thin curves of fresh celery and place sprigs of fresh herbs in any gaps (photo 3). The dish is finished by carefully inserting the thin end of the handle (photo 4). The filled cup will sit more easily on the plate, and survive the journey to the table, if it is gently laid on a further blob of mayonnaise.

1 Start off with a blob of home-made mayonnaise in the base of each cup.

2 Top the mayonnaise with skinned and seeded tomato dice.

3 Top the tomato with avocado, celery and herbs.

4 Carefully insert the pastry handles made from left-over pastry.

Avocado cream

*A*NOTHER TASTY AVOCADO *starter, delicious served with slices of brown yoghurt seed loaf (p. 163).*

Serves 6

2 ripe avocados, skinned, stoned and chopped

juice and finely grated rind of 1 lime

2 tablespoons good-quality cream cheese

2 tablespoons double cream

2 teaspoons runny honey

3 tablespoons natural yoghurt

12 teaspoons sunflower seeds, toasted

Place everything except the sunflower seeds in either a liquidiser or food processor, and blend happily away until smooth. If you do not have one of these machines, the ingredients can be beaten together using an electric hand whisk. Fold in the toasted sunflower seeds and portion into tall glasses. Cover with cling film and leave to chill.

AND TO DRINK

Your favourite Sémillon.

Leek and orange roll

*T*HE LEEK HAS BEEN *considered the most delicate flavoured member of the onion family from the time of Nero – who ate it avidly, apparently, as he thought it improved his singing voice! The Romans probably introduced it to Britain, and it was extremely popular until Mrs Beeton suggested that it smelled too strongly on the breath! The Welsh adopted the leek as their national emblem, and St David was able to distinguish his own men from the enemy in battle as leeks were worn in their hats.*

The leek does, however, have a distinguished history in both haute *and peasant cuisines, as there are many classical French dishes using* poireaux; *everyone knows the famous vichyssoise soup, for one. The vegetable is also an essential ingredient in many national British dishes, notably the delicious Scottish cock-a-leekie.*

For years leeks were thought of as a winter vegetable, widely available in this country from September to early April. Of late, they seem to be on the market in most months. I always select the thinnest leeks on sale as they are invariably more tender, younger and with a higher proportion of white flesh. Make sure that the leaves are fresh and show no sign whatever of wilting. Leeks can be mucky to prepare, and there is always a difference of opinion among cooks over the use of the top green bits. I never serve these but, after cutting them away from the lovely white flesh, I simply wash them thoroughly, chop the strips roughly and use them in vegetable stocks. Another mistake when preparing leeks is to leave them in water hours in advance to clean them thoroughly; the dirt will come out, of course, but so will most of the flavour!

Serves 6 (generously)

1 ½ lb (700 g) white ends of thin fresh leeks

finely grated rind of 4 oranges

4 oz (100 g) softened butter

6 medium eggs, separated

salt and freshly ground black pepper

2 tablespoons finely chopped parsley

To serve

2 oz (50 g) strong Cheddar cheese, finely grated

12 tablespoons natural yoghurt

toasted mixed nuts

Pre-heat your oven to gas mark 4, 350°F (180°C), and lightly butter and flour a Swiss roll tin measuring approximately 8 × 10 in (20 × 25 cm).

Split the leeks in four lengthways and then chop them very finely. If necessary, wash them in cold water, then dry very well. Mix with the grated orange rind.

Melt the butter in a thick-bottomed saucepan and, when sizzling, add the leeks and orange rind. Cook over a medium heat until nice and golden and then, one by one, beat in the egg yolks (photo 1). Add a little salt and pepper, and stir in the chopped parsley.

In a clean bowl, beat the egg whites with a pinch of salt until quite stiff and fold half this mixture into the leek mix (photo 2). When they are thoroughly combined, fold in the balance. This is best and most easily done using a long-handled spoon, held at the end of the handle.

Turn the mixture into the prepared tin and then, using a palette knife, very gently spread it evenly over the base (photo 3). Bake in the pre-heated oven for 25 minutes.

Turn out on to a double thickness of greaseproof paper and sprinkle on the grated cheese. Roll it up by simply taking hold of each corner of the greaseproof paper near you and pulling this up at a 90 degree angle on your work surface (photo 4). The roll will actually roll beautifully away from you.

Cut the roll into rounds and top with the natural yoghurt that has been gently warmed through. It is delicious if scattered with assorted toasted nuts.

Deep-fried curried leek rings

*T*HIS IS ANOTHER SIMPLE WAY to serve leeks either as a vegetable with, say, poached fish, or, for that matter, in place of crisps.

Discard the green end of the leeks and also the root, and then cut the white parts into ⅛ in (3 mm) circles. Put these into a sink half filled with cold water and, using your index finger, force all the circles away from one another. Wash well. Scoop up in a sieve and dry well.

Simply toss in seasoned flour to which you have added a touch of curry powder and then deep-fry in hot oil until golden and crisp. Drain well on kitchen paper before you serve, otherwise they can be rather greasy.

1 Beat the egg yolks one by one into the leeks.

2 Fold half the beaten egg white into the leek mix.

3 Very carefully spread the mixture out in the prepared Swiss roll tin.

4 Take hold of the greaseproof paper, lift up, and the roll will roll up beautifully.

AND TO DRINK

To accompany a first course, I would serve chilled sherry.

Minted pea purée herb slice

*L*AST YEAR OZZIE, *my Old English sheepdog, and I went on holiday in the north of Scotland as I had to write an article for Lloyd's Log on hotels in that part of the world that would accept dogs. It was as happy for Ozzie as it was for me as she thoroughly enjoyed the company of other dogs en route, and I found some splendid hostelries and on the whole dined extremely well. Without any doubt the best food was cooked by Hilary Brown at La Potinière in Gullane, and anybody passing within forty miles of this village should make the detour for a meal. (It's a small restaurant, booked well in advance for weekends, but there are often places for lunch mid-week).*

However, the dish I enjoyed most was cooked by Frances Atkins at Farleyer House Hotel near Aberfeldy, and although she was most reluctant even to discuss the recipe with me, immediately I returned to Miller Howe and the farm I spent ages trying to re-create it. Frankly, I am honest enough to say it isn't quite as good as hers, but it is a smasher and is served at least every ten days at the hotel. We are now experimenting with individual ones lined with smoked trout mousse and topped with horseradish cream and thinly sliced radishes; a rich duck liver pâté one went down a bomb garnished with tangerines and topped with Marsala jelly!

An interesting alternative garnish to the one suggested is samphire, when in season (for a short spell around August). You can buy samphire from good fishmongers. When blanched and then marinated for 24 hours in lemon juice, it makes a splendid contrast to the pea purée base if used instead of the radishes and spring onions.

Using the following slightly adapted recipe for savoury tarts on p. 146, you will have sufficient pastry for three 8–10 in (20–25 cm) loose-bottomed, fluted flan tins. The filling is sufficient for one flan.

Curried savoury pastry

1 lb (450 g) plain flour
pinch of sa!t
2 level tablespoons curry powder
10 oz (275 g) softened butter
2 medium eggs at room temperature

Pea purée

8 oz (225 g) frozen **petits pois,** *defrosted*

pinch of salt

1 teaspoon caster sugar

40 fresh mint leaves (sounds a lot, but you want the flavour to slightly dominate)

5 fl oz (150 ml) double cream

½ oz (15 g) powdered gelatine

5 tablespoons white wine

Garnish

4 radishes, wiped and thinly sliced

6 spring onions, finely chopped

4 tablespoons finely chopped fresh garden herbs

5 fl oz (150 ml) white wine aspic

1 Bake the flan case blind, and check after 30 minutes.

2 Line the base of the cooked flan with the pea purée mixture.

3 Arrange the garnish ingredients on top of the set pea purée.

4 Spoon the aspic over the garnish to complete the dish.

Make up and roll out the pastry as outlined on p. 147 and use to line an 8–10 in (20–25 cm) loose-bottomed flan tin. Put in the fridge to chill and, meanwhile, pre-heat the oven to gas mark 3, 325°F (160°C). Bake the flan blind as instructed for at least 40 minutes – but take a look after 30 minutes to see that all is well (photo 1). Remove from the oven and leave to cool.

For the pea purée, cook the frozen peas in boiling salted water, then drain and leave to go cold. Liquidise or purée the peas with the caster sugar, mint leaves and double cream, making sure that all the mint leaves disappear into the mix. Pass through a coarse sieve into a bowl.

Reconstitute the gelatine with the wine (see p. 129), then pass through a fine sieve and combine with the pea purée. Line the base of your cold cooked flan case with this (photo 2) and leave to set.

When the pea purée has set, arrange the radishes, spring onions and herbs on top of it (photo 3). Make up the aspic following the instructions on the packet, and pass through a fine sieve into a jug. When getting cold and beginning to set, spoon over the herb, radish and onion mix (photo 4).

Leave the slice to cool and set in the fridge, then serve with a substantial salad and home-made mayonnaise (see p. 166).

AND TO DRINK

A glass of good chilled cider will have you licking your lips!

Baked eggs

SO MUCH HAS BEEN WRITTEN and said about eggs of late that one tends to feel slightly bored with the subject. The scare of 1988 does, however, seem to be over, but it made me think, and worry momentarily. Then I realised that the eggs I get, both in the Lakes and at the farm in the Rossendale valley, are fresh and free-range; the hens spend their days out in the fields and lanes pecking away at the things Mother Nature intended them to eat, not the dried fish or cornmeal the poor, sad battery creatures are stuffed with.

The current EC rules state that eggs, when packed, have to have the boxes stamped with the appropriate date of packing (no hint of when they were laid!). And reliable supermarkets are now very stringent about checking the shelf-life of their products. However, true free-range eggs may, from time to time, include an old egg which the hen has cunningly laid in a different hiding place, so that it was not found and collected immediately. To be on the safe side, test your eggs for age by putting each one in a bowl of cold water. If they remain horizontal at the bottom, all is well; if they tilt slightly, they are not so fresh; and if they literally rise to the top, throw them away.

Most recipes call for medium-sized eggs which should give you approximately 2 oz (50 g) white and yolk to use. I keep my eggs in the cold of the outside garage, and always bring them in the night before I plan to have a good old-fashioned baking session. A lot of people insist on storing them in the fridge, but most manufacturers these days place the egg compartment next to the coldest part, which, in my opinion, does the eggs no good.

I always associate eggs with Easter. In my very young days it was a time, even during the war, for chocolate Easter eggs; these were rolled down the banks of the amphitheatre at Furness Abbey on Easter Sunday morning, and only when they

broke going downhill were they eaten. There were also Simnel cakes, hot cross buns, easterledge puddings and hard-boiled eggs painstakingly decorated and displayed on the parlour window-ledge for all and sundry to see (along with the newly starched net curtains and ruffled double-width window curtains, dressed to the street and not to the room!).

On Easter Sunday now I invariably serve one of the following recipes for breakfast. I always have masses of daffodils on the table too — that burst of gold immediately brings joy to the day.

Pre-heat the oven to gas mark 5, 375°F (190°C), and paint the base and sides of individual 3 in (7.5 cm) ramekins liberally with melted butter. Lay on the base of each a few pieces of smoked salmon or smoked haddock (if using the latter, add ½ teaspoon grated cheese for an even better flavour). Break a medium egg on top. Put the ramekins in a roasting tray and pour a little boiling water around them. Cook in the pre-heated oven for 12–15 minutes, depending on how you like your eggs done. Serve on a doileyed saucer with a teaspoon, and of course have plenty of toast soldiers to hand.

Soft-boiled eggs with Keta

*K*ETA IS AMERICAN *red salmon caviar roe, available at most major food stores. Lumpfish roe can also be used. Allow two eggs per person, and have them at room temperature before you start to cook.*

There are two important things to remember when boiling eggs: first, they should not have room to roll around in the saucepan; and second, the water should never rapidly boil, but swiftly simmer.

Using a tablespoon, lower each egg gently into the compact saucepan as the water starts to simmer swiftly; it will momentarily cease bubbling, but as soon as it starts to do so again, cook the eggs for just over 3 minutes, then remove with the same tablespoon.

Using a teaspoon, take off the tops of the eggs and scoop out the cooked insides into a small dish. Swiftly chop together, then return to the main egg shell. (There will be a little egg left over, but domestic pets need a Sunday celebration too!) Put ½ teaspoon Keta on top of each portion and serve at once in egg cups with triangles of brown bread spread with butter mixed with a little lemon juice.

AND TO DRINK

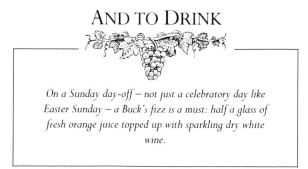

On a Sunday day-off — not just a celebratory day like Easter Sunday — a Buck's fizz is a must: half a glass of fresh orange juice topped up with sparkling dry white wine.

Baked cob containers

*D*INNER COB ROLLS, *after a couple of days, invariably become hard, but never discard them as they make ideal containers for all sorts of left-over foods – particularly the buttered eggs below – and they will store, when baked, in an air-tight container for at least a week.*

A 'cube' should be made of each round cob by cutting four straight sides and then nicking off the top. The discarded sides may go to the birds, but keep the top and then, using a small, very sharp knife, hollow out a square or circle from the middle (photo 1).

Submerge the hollowed-out shapes and lids in melted butter and place on a baking tray in a pre-heated oven at gas mark 4, 350°F (180°C). Bake for at least 1 hour, when the containers will be brown and crisp (photo 2). Lids only take 15 minutes. When needed, they should be warmed through, stuffed with any one of a number of different fillings: mince (see p. 84) perhaps, or a little cheese and herb pâté (see p. 16), in the middle and then a quail or bantam egg baked on top of this. A filling made up of the cheese topping for the savoury cheese peach on p. 22 is very satisfying. A few prawns or some smoked salmon in the cream sauce on p. 164 makes a very upmarket version of this dish. Baked beans with finely diced apple and a few sultanas, or a mixture of banana, walnut and dates can also be put in the hole and baked. Experiment!

Buttered eggs

*T*HESE ARE PARTICULARLY *delicious when served inside a warmed prepared cob as above, or on a slice of hot, buttered toast.*

Per person

1 large fresh egg
salt and freshly ground black pepper
2 oz (50 g) butter
1 level teaspoon chopped fresh herbs (tops of bulb fennel, parsley or chives)

Break the egg into a mixing bowl and lightly beat it, adding a pinch of salt and a generous grinding of pepper.

1 Square the sides of the cobs and hollow them out.

2 Bake the buttery cob containers until brown and crisp.

3 Add chopped fresh herbs to the buttered eggs while they are still runny.

4 For the baked savoury eggs, finely slice the onion and red pepper (removing seeds and pith from the latter).

Baked savoury eggs

*T*HIS AND THE OTHER *two recipes on the page are relatively cheap, cheerful and chirpy, resembling the kind of homely grub I have on the occasional night when I am in by myself at the farm. These evenings are equally relished by my Old English sheepdog, as not only does she have my undivided attention for several hours, but she also gets to lick up all the left-overs from the pans. She must be one of the most spoiled gourmand canines in existence!*

Serves 2

4–6 oz (100–175 g) red pepper (prepared weight)

1 tablespoon olive oil

1 oz (25 g) butter

1 fat garlic clove, crushed with 1 teaspoon salt

6 oz (175 g) onions, peeled and finely sliced

1 teaspoon caster sugar

1 oz (25 g) strong cheese, finely grated

2 medium eggs

generous scattering of freshly ground coriander seeds or black pepper

Melt half the butter in a small saucepan and, when it begins to 'bubble', pour in the beaten egg and stir continuously with a wooden spoon. As it begins to thicken, add the rest of the butter. Do not overcook.

Take the saucepan off the heat while the egg is still runny (photo 3) and add the herbs. Serve as you wish (see introduction).

Pre-heat the oven to gas mark 4, 350°F (180°C), and have ready two deep ovenproof saucers or dishes.

Cut the pepper in half, discard the seeds and slice very thinly (photo 4). Heat the oil in a frying-pan and add the butter. Cook the prepared garlic, onions, pepper and sugar over a medium heat for 10 minutes.

Divide the pepper and onions between the two dishes, making a slight hollow in the middle of the mix. Scatter over the cheese and break an egg into each hollow. Be fairly generous with the coriander (or black pepper, if you are using that). Bake in the pre-heated oven for 10–12 minutes.

AND TO DRINK

If you want to pamper yourself even further, I would drink with these egg dishes a wine made from a Chardonnay or Sémillon grape from the New World.

Toasted sandwiches

*M*OST AMERICAN HOTELS *excel themselves when it comes to toasted sandwiches, and in my opinion your bedroom is the only place to eat them — the portions are huge and practically impossible to eat in a civilised fashion. I often resort to devouring them in the bath. Hotels serve at least a three-layered tier of toast — frequently four-layered. The fillings are usually based on turkey, bacon, mayonnaise and salad.*

I must admit I prefer mine to be made in the small toasted sandwich machines available from most electrical shops. Whatever you do, avoid the cotton-wool sliced gunge that is sold as bread — support a real local baker. And if you want an American professional type of sandwich, it's worth going to the trouble of grilling one side of each slice to be used. Then place the filling on this grilled side, with the other toasted side on top, and finish it off in your machine.

Lay the half-toasted slices of bread on the work surface and lightly spread the toasted sides with butter. Put your filling (see opposite) in the middle and gently spread it out towards the edges, leaving ¼ in (5 mm) space all round (photo 1). Place the other slice of bread on top and use a rolling pin to press the edges together (photo 2). Put the sandwich into your machine only when the latter is hot and ready (normally when the red light goes out). You will need to get to know your machine for the length of time needed, and this also varies with the type of bread you use too (photo 3).

You can also make up sandwiches, wrap them completely in tinfoil (photo 4) and cook them on a barbecue. At an average heat they take about 10 minutes.

Commercial establishments normally serve toasted sandwiches on thinly sliced iceberg lettuce, but I prefer the stronger texture and taste of watercress.

Radish flowers dried and dipped in a little coarse sea salt provide a delightful contrast in texture (see p. 111), and once upon a time I would have hailed the cherry tomatoes. Nowadays, however, these too often appear to be so forced that they are devoid of flavour.

Most toasted sandwiches can be enhanced with a piece of apple – simply wipe the fruit clean, cut into four, leaving the skin on, and remove the core. Add generous sprigs of parsley too, if you like.

FILLINGS

A sandwich made from a piece of bread 4 × 3 in (10 × 7.5 cm) needs approximately 2 oz (50 g) filling.

CHEESE, ONION, TOMATO AND EGG

Without any doubt this is my favourite, and it will sharpen any jaded appetite. Combine a lightly beaten egg with grated strong Cheddar cheese and a generous hint of Dijon mustard, adding finely sliced spring onions or chives, and top with sliced tomatoes.

SALMON MAYONNAISE WITH DICED CUCUMBER

Tinned salmon, turned out into a bowl and well mashed, should be mixed with home-made mayonnaise (see p. 166) and finely diced cucumber. (Split the cucumber in two and remove the seeds first.) A touch of wine vinegar will give it a kick, and you could substitute finely diced fennel for the cucumber, as this will give a crunch to the mix.

TUNA FISH

This can be done as above, but use finely diced red pepper instead of cucumber.

CHICKEN AND AVOCADO

A cold roast chicken carcass will give you a lot of meat if painstakingly stripped. Mix with diced avocado and Worcestershire sauce.

LEFT-OVERS

No sensible household throws away left-overs and these, more often than not, can combine to make very interesting sandwich fillings. Breakfast left-overs are particularly useful – black pudding thinly sliced and painted with a little mustard; sausages sliced and coated with chutney; mushroom caps, squashy fried tomatoes and bacon (best put back in the oven to make it really crisp and then broken up). Remember: waste not, want not.

1 Spread the toasted side of the bread with butter and filling, leaving a ¼ in (5 mm) border.

2 Put on the top of your sandwich and press down on the edges firmly with a rolling pin.

3 Place in your sandwich toaster until done – you'll need to follow the manufacturer's instructions.

4 You can also wrap sandwiches in tinfoil and cook them over barbecue coals.

AND TO DRINK

Whether having a toasted sandwich as supper, lunch or snack, I would accompany it with beer or Guinness.

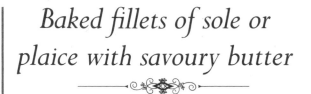

Baked fillets of sole or plaice with savoury butter

*T*HIS IS A VERY SIMPLE *dish — simple to prepare, cook and serve. You must, however, use fresh fish. Frozen fillets are just not the same: they are frozen one on top of another, and so all that lovely springy flesh is firmly pressed down and the texture is destroyed.*

If you are cooking this as a fish course, you will need, per person, a piece of fillet weighing 3 oz (75 g) before skinning, giving you a 2 oz (50 g) portion. For a main course, an 8 oz (225 g) fillet is required.

Per person

1 sole or plaice fillet

savoury breadcrumbs (see opposite)

butter

Garnish

1 sprig of parsley

1 savoury butter circle (see opposite)

1 slice lemon

Pre-heat the oven to gas mark 4, 350°F (180°C).

Skinning fish is fairly easy, but you *must* use a sharp, serrated knife. The first time you perform this task, you should do it slowly. Place the fillet skin-side down on your work surface (photo 1) and, holding the tail end between thumb and forefinger, carefully cut the flesh away from you, letting it roll over on itself.

Coat the damp, skinned fish on both sides with savoury breadcrumbs (photo 2); if you fancy a richer dish, dip the fillets in melted butter first. Lay each coated fillet on a well-buttered baking tray and cover with cling film (photo 3) until you are ready to cook.

Remove the cling film and bake in the pre-heated

*F*ISH

1 To skin fillets of any kind of fish, a sharp knife is essential.

2 Coat the fish generously with savoury breadcrumbs.

3 Lay the fillets on a buttered tray, cover with cling film and chill until you are ready to cook.

oven for 15 minutes if serving fish-course portions; or for at least 20 minutes if using as a main course.

Serve on hot plates garnished with parsley, and a savoury butter circle (main picture) on a lemon slice.

Savoury butter circles

*N*O FRIDGE OR FREEZER *should be without a couple of sausage-like 8 oz (225 g) savoury butters, as they add a different taste to so many dishes – the baked fish in the recipe above, any grilled meat and quite a few steamed vegetables, for example.*

Simply whisk 8 oz (225 g) softened butter to a fluffy texture and then incorporate *one* of the following:

4 garlic cloves, skinned and crushed with ¹/₂ teaspoon salt

1 heaped tablespoon grated horseradish, creamed with 2 pinches of white pepper and a little salt

juice and finely grated rind of 1 lemon or lime

2 tablespoons tomato purée with a pinch each of salt and caster sugar

1 heaped tablespoon wholegrain mustard

Place a piece of tinfoil on the work surface and a piece of good-quality greaseproof paper on top of this. Spread the butter on the paper and roll it up in the shape of a sausage. Chill, and then cut off circles as required.

Savoury breadcrumbs

4 oz (100 g) stale bread

1 oz (25 g) stale cheese

1 spring onion, trimmed

4 large sprigs fresh parsley

pinch of dry English mustard

Simply whizz all the ingredients together in your food processor.

AND TO DRINK

A wine made from the Sauvignon Blanc grape is a must, and once again I go for those from the New World. The Hawkes Bay Sauvignon Blancs from New Zealand are masterpieces, and my outright favourite is Mission Sémillon Sauvignon Blanc 1985.

Fillet of sole
with banana and cream

*S*OLE MUST BE the most versatile of all the fish found in the seas of Europe, and it has featured in many classic dishes over the centuries. Its flesh is firm and white, and its distinctive flavour actually improves after a couple of days, whereas most fish are reckoned to be better cooked and eaten straight out of the water. The name Dover sole is really a patriotic myth, implying that the fish is found only at its best in this part of the English Channel.

Sole simply grilled, served with wedges of lemon and deep-fried parsley or a home-made tartare sauce, is food fit for the gods. Because it is readily available for most of the year, the fish forms the basis of many of our dishes at Miller Howe. Sole can be used in soufflés and terrines; it can be cut into strips, coated with coarse coconut flakes and deep-fried (like the cod on p. 54); it can be baked with any number of coatings; or casseroled with grapes and wine. The permutations are endless. And with most sole dishes you will find that the preparation can be done in advance, leaving just the final cooking to be done immediately before the meal.

I like comforting, self-indulgent food, and this recipe is very much in that style. Whenever I am entertaining at the farm, I find, more and more, that a small fish course between a starter and main course is much appreciated by the guests, and is no trouble at all to cook and serve. In fact, while we are eating the dish, the vegetables for the main course are steaming away (see p. 94), and are cooked to perfection!

Some people might be somewhat surprised that here I am combining this delicate fish with banana, cream and Parmesan cheese – but don't reject the idea until you've tried it!

The fish should be filleted and skinned, and it goes without saying that it should be fresh. When buying fish, don't be afraid to touch it. The body should be firm to the touch, and it shouldn't have a strong fishy smell. The gills should be moist and, even more important, the eyes should stand out brightly. Dull, sunken eyes are a sign of old stock.

The following quantities are for one serving. Garlic lovers could add a hint of crushed garlic to the breadcrumb, cheese and parsley topping. Serve with thinly sliced, thickly buttered brown bread — and, if you have time, beat some fresh lemon juice into the butter.

Per person

butter

salt and freshly ground black pepper

1 × 3–4 oz (75–100 g) sole fillet, skinned

¼ banana, peeled

2 tablespoons single cream

½ tablespoon fresh breadcrumbs

½ tablespoon grated Parmesan cheese

1 level teaspoon chopped fresh parsley, plus extra to garnish

1 Have ready buttered ramekins, then wrap each sole fillet round ¼ banana.

2 Place the wrapped fish in a ramekin and cover with cream.

Prepare the dish in an individual ramekin which can be taken out of the oven and put straight on to a serving plate. Lightly butter the ramekin and season with salt and pepper.

Wrap the fillet of fish around the banana (photo 1), and place it snugly in the ramekin. Cover with the cream (photo 2). If not cooking the dish immediately, place the ramekin in a suitable roasting tin, cover with cling film and leave in the fridge.

When ready to cook, pre-heat the oven to gas mark 4, 350°F (180°C). Pour hot water into the roasting tin to come half way up the sides of the ramekin (photo 3). Bake in the pre-heated oven for 15 minutes.

Heat the grill to high. Mix together the breadcrumbs, cheese and parsley, and sprinkle over the sole (photo 4). Flash under the grill until it begins to brown and bubble. Garnish with extra parsley if you like.

3 Place the ramekins in a roasting tin and pour in sufficient hot water to come half-way up their sides.

4 After baking, sprinkle each ramekin with breadcrumbs, cheese and parsley, before flashing under the grill.

AND TO DRINK

I would choose an old favourite — a buttery New World Chardonnay.

Smoked haddock with bacon bits in cream cheese sauce

*H*ADDOCK IS A FAVOURITE *fish of mine as it is so versatile and relatively inexpensive. The unsmoked white fish is particularly delicious if marinated for 24 hours in a liberal coating of natural yoghurt and then simply baked in the oven at gas mark 4, 350°F (180°C), for approximately 15 minutes. It is also good steamed, and better still if deep-fried in a beer batter.*

However, when it is smoked, haddock comes into its own. There are rogues about, though, who sell smoked haddock which hasn't in fact been smoked at all, but simply chemically treated and dyed. Scotland is the only place in the world where this fish is smoked properly, particularly in Findon near Aberdeen (pronounced Finnan, incidentally!), and at Auchmithie near Arbroath. Arbroath smokies are gutted and closed up prior to hot-smoking, and the Finnan haddies are cold-smoked when split open. Seek out a reliable local fishmonger and explain your needs, or else buy quite a lot when you find a good source and freeze the surplus. I normally freeze haddock after lightly poaching it in milk, and then portioning the flakes into 4 oz (100 g) plastic containers; these can quickly be made up thereafter in various ways.

I often enjoy haddock dishes for a TV tray supper, but my real idea of heaven on a day off is to have my fresh morning orange juice and cuppa in bed reading the papers, then to come down and cook this dish, gilding the lily with a couple of poached farm eggs and lots of piping hot, lavishly buttered toast. As all the preparation can be done the night before, it takes only about 5 or 10 minutes to have the finished dish on the table.

Both smoked haddock and smoked bacon are quite salty, which is why I always poach the fish first in milk. (This milk, strained, can be stored or frozen in a container and then used at a later stage to make a white sauce to go with a plain fish.)

Serves 4

1 lb (450 g) smoked haddock fillet

10 fl oz (300 ml) cold milk

4 large sprigs of fresh parsley

4 circles from an onion slice

12 black peppercorns

4 oz (100 g) smoked bacon, de-rinded

1 tablespoon olive oil

10 fl oz (300 ml) double cream

4 oz (100 g) strong Cheddar cheese, grated

Garnish

croûtons baked in melted butter

4 large sprigs of parsley, deep-fried

Pre-heat the oven to gas mark 4, 350°F (180°C), and have ready a dish that will snugly hold the fish, enabling it to be covered with the milk.

Put the cold milk, sprigs of parsley, onion circles and peppercorns in the dish. Lay the fish skin-side up in this and cook in the pre-heated oven for 20 minutes. Remove from the oven and, when the fish is cold, take it out of the dish and carefully remove large flakes of flesh from the skin, taking great care to throw away any bones. Leave to one side.

Cut the bacon up fairly small with either sharp kitchen scissors or a good sharp knife and fry it in the olive oil until extremely well cooked and crisp (photo 1). Remove and drain on a double thickness of kitchen paper. Leave to one side.

When you wish to serve the dish, allow 10 minutes for the next stage. Reduce the double cream by half in the pan in which you cooked the bacon, and add the cheese to make a very thick sauce. Simply stir in the smoked haddock flakes (photo 2), and cook for a few minutes until well warmed through, then fold in the cold crisp bacon. Portion into four warmed serving dishes.

It all goes much further if you accompany each portion with a 'heart'-shaped croûton (photo 3) which has been liberally dipped in melted butter and then baked in the oven alongside the fish.

Deep-fried parsley is a joy, too, as a final garnish. However, you must be careful that the parsley is bone dry before frying. As you put it in the hot fat it will bubble and sizzle quite loudly (photo 4), and the minute the noise stops the parsley is ready: it takes only seconds. Drain well on kitchen paper.

1 Fry the bacon bits in olive oil until crisp.

2 Stir the cooked haddock flakes into the thick cream and cheese sauce.

3 Cut bread into 'heart' shaped croûtons, dip in melted butter and bake in the oven alongside the fish.

4 Dry parsley sprigs very thoroughly before deep-frying – for seconds only.

AND TO DRINK

If eating this as a supper dish, a cool Chenin Blanc complements it very nicely.

Deep-fried coconut cod steaks

*T*HERE ARE TIMES *when I despair of all the bungling bureaucrats in Brussels. My heart sank some time ago at the plight of the Cornish fishermen who, having spent arduous hours at sea, had to throw most of their catch back because EC regulations categorically state that cod is a cold-water fish and can be caught only in northern waters.*

It has been proved time and time again that big is not best – we small businessmen, and our customers, know only too well

that when a local branch is taken over by a larger one, efficiency and service fly out of the window. And this is no less true of bureaucracy. So I hope that sanity will soon prevail and that the fine fishermen of the south may be allowed to land their cod. When they do, this is a delicious way of serving it.

In many homes the electric deep-fryer has superseded the old-fashioned chip pan, and of course bottled cooking oil is usually used in place of the delicious beef dripping which, in my childhood days, was the only choice for this type of cooking. I recall a fish and chip shop in Arnold, Nottingham, which opened its doors only when the vast steel cooking pans full of beef dripping, and heated over open coke fires, were sufficiently hot. Nowadays, I suspect, if the fire brigade didn't close the shop, the health and safety officer certainly would!

Serves 4

4 × 4 oz (100 g) cod steaks, boned and skinned

3 oz (75 g) seasoned flour

2 small eggs, lightly beaten

3 oz (75 g) large-flake coconut (not **desiccated**)

vegetable oil for deep-frying

Garnish

lemon wedges

sprigs of parsley

1 Dip the cod steaks in seasoned flour.

2 Coat the floured steaks in beaten egg and then in large-flake coconut.

3 For deep-frying, use either an electric deep-frier (built-in like mine, or free-standing), or a deep-frying pan with a removable basket.

4 Drain the fried cod very well on kitchen paper to ensure that it is dry and crisp.

Dry the fish with kitchen paper and coat in seasoned flour (photo 1). Dip the floured fish into the beaten eggs and then coat with as many pieces of coconut as possible (photo 2).

Whether you elect to cook the fish in an electric deep-frier or on top of the stove (photo 3), it is best to do so in two stages: first, deep-fry for 5 minutes at a lower temperature to part cook, and then for 3 minutes in very hot oil to complete the cooking and brown the outside. If the temperature is too hot at the outset, the outside gets overcooked long before the actual inside of the fish is ready. And if you do use a saucepan and a chip basket, do remember *never* to leave the handle poking out over the stove edge when cooking, as a knocked-over pan of hot bubbling fat causes more harm and injury than anything else in the kitchen: watch the pan like a hawk.

After frying, drain the fish well on a double thickness of kitchen paper to absorb surplus fat and retain the crispness of the coating (photo 4). Serve, garnish and eat immediately.

AND TO DRINK

A delicious New World Chenin Blanc.

Steamed fish

SEVERAL YEARS AGO a large, well-known, kitchen-equipment manufacturer brought out a rather sophisticated, commercial steam oven, and this became the rage of its time. Fellow chefs extolled its virtues, sales personnel bombarded me with telephone calls and literature, each catering magazine carried larger and larger ads, and as my staff and I travelled round the world, we saw these stainless-steel monsters in many kitchens. I was put off them immediately. They were mainly used for the pre-cooking of many dishes which could then be 'plated' or 'flatted' to order and 'finished off' either in the steamer or microwave oven. Very few chefs seemed actually to have sat down and thought out a new way of cooking their old recipes in the oven in order to improve their texture and flavour. It was this oven which introduced the craze for half-moon side dishes with a 'Restaurant Selection of Fresh Seasonal Vegetables from the Market'. Fresh they might have been that morning, but with a double cooking they were pretty to look at but pretty tasteless to eat.

However, two years ago I was given a super stainless-steel steamer by some friends. It sat on the window ledge for a few weeks until the yen for using it struck me. Then I fell in love with it. Steaming is quick, simple and above all healthy, and is ideally suited to many ingredients, not just fish (see below and also on p. 94).

The basic point to remember when using this equipment is that any food to be cooked by this method requires extra flavouring and seasoning, as it is being cooked literally in a steam-bath. Anybody with an aversion to salt should find this method ideal − to add flavour they should simply be more generous with any fresh herbs that will complement the dish. You must also experiment with putting spices, oils, mustards, vinegars and herbs in the water.

For those not wanting to splash out on yet another piece of equipment, a colander resting in a large saucepan and covered with a tight-fitting lid (photo 1) makes an acceptable substitute.

The method of steaming, which is the same for all ingredients, is as follows. Half-fill the base of the steamer (or saucepan) with cold water and season liberally with free-flowing salt and freshly ground black pepper. Put the lid on and bring to the boil over a high heat. Very quickly remove the lid and with

equal speed set over the bubbling water your colander or tray containing the prepared food. Put the lid back on at once and cook for the exact time required. It is better that your guests wait for food then that the food waits for the guests.

FILLET OF HALIBUT OR COD

A 4 oz (100 g) fillet of halibut or cod measuring 4 × 3 × ¾ in (10 × 7.5 × 2 cm) takes 5 minutes to cook. Underneath the fillet place a very thin round of fresh root ginger (this is easily preserved in sherry, by the way: see photo 2). On the fillet place a thin circle of lemon on which you have put 1 oz (25 g) softened butter (photo 3).

SALMON

A 4 oz (100 g) piece of salmon, boned and skinned, laid on either fresh fennel or dill (photo 3) with a thin piece of skinned lime on top, then seasoned, takes 6 minutes to cook.

SCAMPI AND SCALLOPS

Scampi sprinkled with grated fresh root ginger and the grated rind and juice of a lime takes 4 minutes to steam. Scallops, first marinated overnight in something like Kümmel, with lots of fresh herbs, can be steamed for 10 minutes by themselves or wrapped in blanched lettuce leaves.

Meats can be steamed very successfully as well.

BREAST OF CHICKEN

A portion of boned chicken breast usually weighs about 4 oz (100 g). It can be marinated for up to 5 days in white wine or natural yoghurt provided it is in a tightly closed container in the fridge. To cook, place fresh herbs on the base of the steamer, season the chicken breast well and lay it on top; alternatively sprinkle finely chopped herbs over the chicken (photo 4). Put 1 oz (25 g) butter on each breast, and steam for 10 minutes. The breasts will be succulently moist, but I then 'flash fry' them in a frying-pan of sizzling butter to seal them.

FILLET OF PORK

A 4 oz (100 g) fillet of pork takes 10 minutes to cook, and the flavour is enhanced if you make three small slits and push in thin slivers of preserved ginger; or try an anise star under each portion.

1 A 'home-made' steamer (using a colander, pan and lid) and a new-fangled, 'proper' one.

2 Peeled fresh root ginger, cut into rounds, can be deliciously preserved in a screw top jar of sherry.

3 A halibut steak (right) and a salmon steak (left), ready prepared for steaming in the main picture.

4 Finely chopped fresh herbs add flavour to steamed food.

AND TO DRINK

For the fish — or indeed the chicken or pork — try a chilled Sémillon-Chardonnay blend.

Baked fish in yoghurt

THE MAXIM 'PREPARE BEFORE, cook later' is one I constantly apply to my cooking, as anything to make entertaining easier instantly appeals to me.

Yoghurt is a wonderful food when used for marinating — particularly if you extend the essential 24 hours to 48 or, better still, 72 — provided, of course, your fish is lovely and fresh. You might well ask, 'Why harp on about using fresh fish if it is going to be left around for 3 days in the yoghurt?' The answer is that it will be left in an air-tight container in the fridge smothered with the yoghurt, which will work its way through the fibre of its flesh, making it even more succulent and smooth.

Yes, yoghurt does normally 'split' at a temperature in excess of 350°F (180°C), and some food writers do suggest a touch of cornflour to help stabilise it, but actually the splitting during cooking makes the yoghurt even thicker and creamier when the whey goes runny.

A recent holiday on a small Greek island reminded me how marvellous true local Greek yoghurt is. I was soon revived early each morning with a dish of the silky, creamy, thick yoghurt over which runny Greek honey was dribbled! If you find a reliable local supplier of Greek yoghurt, use him: don't be content with simply settling for the most conveniently bought

product. Shop around. You could even get involved in the home-made yoghurt cult.

One of the toppings I suggest here should suit your palate, but the joy of this particular dish is the endless variations you can concoct from items in your store cupboard or fridge: avocado with tomato and fresh basil; thinly sliced onion rings with capers; banana circles and nuts; pineapple with preserved ginger; gooseberry purée with elderflower; pear quarters, peeled, cored and fanned, sprinkled with a little grated orange rind and savoury breadcrumbs (see p. 49); or finely diced red pepper, apple and celery as here. Go on — experiment!

Per person

4 oz (100 g) piece of halibut, haddock or cod, measuring 3 × 2½ in (7.5 × 6 cm), boned

butter

salt and freshly ground black pepper

at least 2 tablespoons natural yoghurt

Topping

½ tablespoon natural yoghurt mixed with ingredients of your choice (see above)

coarsely grated cheese

Optional garnish

chopped fresh mint, fennel, dill or tarragon

Marinate the fish either in an air-tight container or in the dish in which you are eventually going to cook it. If you opt for the latter, make sure that you liberally grease the base of the dish with butter before putting in the fish and cover the filled dish with a double thickness of cling film. Sprinkle the fish with salt and pepper to taste, then cover with the yoghurt (photo 1). Leave for 24 hours or up to 3 days in the fridge.

When you wish to cook the fish, pre-heat the oven to gas mark 6, 400°F (200°C). Mix together your chosen topping ingredients (except for the cheese) – in photo 2 I have used finely diced red pepper, apple and celery – and cover the fish with the mixture. Bake in the oven for 15 minutes, after which the dish will look rather messy (photo 3). Remove it from the oven, sprinkle with coarsely grated cheese and finish off under a hot grill (photo 4). The finished fish should

then be quickly transferred to warmed serving plates and brought to the table.

A sprinkling of fresh herbs would not go amiss – mint, fennel, dill, tarragon – and the only accompaniment you really need is a lightly dressed green salad as in the main photograph.

1 Coat the fish with natural yoghurt, then leave in the fridge for up to 3 days.

2 Add the topping – here red pepper, apple and celery dice mixed with more yoghurt.

3 After baking for 15 minutes, the fish can look rather messy.

4 Sprinkle with grated cheese and finish off under a hot grill.

AND TO DRINK

I recommend a white wine made from the Sauvignon grape, tasting of new-mown hay and tangy gooseberries. At the moment those from New Zealand are good value.

Halibut stuffed with Gorgonzola and baked in spinach

*O*NE OF MY FAVOURITE *restaurants in New York is the Russian Tea Room, provided one can get a table on the ground floor; the service there seems to be quicker, the food better, and celebrities are more in evidence than upstairs. If I am flying back to the UK that evening, I always order* blinis *with Keta (American salmon caviar roe) and soured cream, but if I am taking a full meal, it has to be the chicken Kiev — the outside is beautifully crisp, the flesh so tender, and the garlic butter pops out liberally when the portion is cut into.*

Now, halibut is my favourite fish, and Gorgonzola one of my favourite cheeses, and to try, as I did, to do to fish what the Russian Tea Room does to chicken with garlic butter proved an impossible task. However, by enclosing each stuffed fish steak in a poached spinach leaf and then gently steaming, I found the salty cheese worked wonders with the delicate flesh of the halibut and all was firmly held in place by the spinach. Accompany this with cider sauce, or with a cream sauce flavoured with mushroom pâté (see pp. 164 and 27) or garden herbs, and you are in for an experience. It's also delicious served on a home-made tomato sauce (see p. 35).

If you find Gorgonzola cheese too strong for your taste, use cheese and herb pâté (see p. 16) instead.

Once again, the beauty of the dish is that all the slog can be done in the morning, and all you have to do at night is to steam the fish and make the sauce. It needs only a lightly dressed green salad as accompaniment (although I gild the lily by adding to this coarsely chopped, soft-boiled eggs!).

Serves 4

4 × 6 oz (175 g) flat halibut steaks, boned and skinned

salt and freshly ground black pepper

4 oz (100 g) Gorgonzola cheese, worked to a cream

*4 large spinach leaves, stalks removed and blanched for
2–3 minutes in lightly salted boiling water*

Lay the fish steaks on the work surface and lightly
season with salt and pepper (photo 1). Into the middle
of each one pipe the creamed Gorgonzola (photo 2),
then fold one half of the steak over the other. Unroll
the blanched spinach leaves, which will have curled up
during blanching (photo 3), and wrap each fish steak in
a leaf (photo 4). All this preparation can be done in
advance and the finished portions stored, covered with
cling film, in a cold larder or the fridge.

If you have invested in a steamer – and I hope you
have as they're invaluable (see p. 56) – bring salted
water to the boil in the base. Put the wrapped fish
portions in the perforated top and steam them for 12
minutes. They are now ready to take to the table, but
will be notably enhanced by the following cider sauce.

Cider sauce

❧ ❧ ❧

*T*HE BASIC REDUCTION *for this can be made in the
morning, and then it takes only minutes to finish off.*

10 fl oz (300 ml) good-quality cider

2 oz (50 g) softened butter, cut in 4 pieces

In a small saucepan, boil the cider to reduce by half,
then put to one side.

When you put the fish on to cook, bring the
reduced cider back up to boiling point and remove
from the heat. Drop in the pieces of butter and shake
the pan until they dissolve. This makes a very runny
sauce, but is absolutely delicious when poured over
each portion of cooked fish.

1 Lay the halibut steaks
on the work surface and
season lightly.

2 Pipe the creamed
cheese into the middle
of each steak.

3 After blanching and
cooling, unroll the
spinach leaves.

4 Wrap each stuffed fish
steak in a spinach leaf.

AND TO DRINK

A wine made from the Sauvignon grape.

Fried monkfish cubes with pineapple and sesame

*M*ONKFISH USED TO BE KNOWN *as angler fish in my early days. It was sold once as 'scampi', but has now become very popular with chefs because of its firm texture. The price has shot up as a result, and it is no longer cheap to buy. Each year I spend a few days with friends in Portree on the Isle of Skye and, being creatures of habit, on the first day we always end up walking down to the harbour to see the fishing boats come in, and buy this fish. Invariably it costs more on the harbourside than I pay at my local fishmonger in Rawtenstall! Each year we do the same, each year I cook it this way, each year we pass the same remark: 'Oh, we did enjoy that!'*

This is a dish that I normally cook for friends who are at ease in the kitchen, because it needs to be served out of the frying-pan on to the plates without a break. On such occasions, I serve guests individual plates of canapés and then beakers of hot soup while they hang around the large conservatory kitchen: the evening is always extremely informal and friendly. Though the monkfish cubes are fried in this recipe, they are also ideal for the steamer method of cooking (see p. 56).

When buying the monkfish for this recipe, you will have to ask the fishmonger for the weight you need off the bone. (Photos 1 and 2 show the head being removed then the flesh being taken off the single thick bone.) Monkfish is a rather large, ugly fish, but the enormous head, mouth and solid backbone make up for a lot of waste overall; it is the tail only that is fleshy, and this is filleted.

I like to use my garlic oil for frying the monkfish cubes, and this can be easily made when you have 15 minutes or so to spare. Take any old, but perfectly clean, 1 lb (450 g) screw-top jar (chutney jars are particularly useful) and place in the bottom at least 12 cloves of fresh garlic that have been topped, tailed and peeled. Pour good-quality olive oil over these, right up to the rim of the jar. Put the cap on, secure tightly, and leave in a cool, dark place for at least a fortnight. You will be surprised at how strong the oil tastes. It is ideal for

frying off small croûtons for certain soups, or for pan-frying sirloin steaks. (If you have kept the red pepper oil from the recipe for baked red pepper on p. 28, you could also use this for the fish.)

Serves 2

8 oz (225 g) monkfish (boned weight)

2 tablespoons plain flour

2 teaspoons dry English mustard

4 tablespoons garlic oil or red pepper oil (see above)

To serve

2 dessertspoons sesame seeds

2 × ½ in (1 cm) thick slices fresh pineapple

sprigs of fresh coriander or parsley

Divide the fish into two 4 oz (100 g) portions and cut each one into five even-sized pieces. Mix the flour and mustard powder together and coat the pieces of fish liberally with this. Set aside.

Pre-heat the oven to gas mark 4, 350°F (180°C). Spread out the sesame seeds on an ungreased baking tray in the pre-heated oven for 20 minutes or until they are lightly browned. Cut each pineapple slice into five cubes the same size as the fish pieces (photo 3), place on a separate well buttered baking tray and heat through in the oven for 15 minutes. Ensure that the sesame seeds and pineapple cubes are ready before you start to cook the fish.

In a frying-pan approximately 10 in (25 cm) in diameter, heat the oil. When you pan-fry fish like this, the desired result is a fairly 'crisp' outside and a soft, succulent and tasty inside. To achieve this, you must not put the fish pieces in until the oil is actually 'singing' to you. And if you overcrowd the pan, the heat will be quickly and considerably reduced, so your fish will boil and steam in the fat rather than 'broil' and seal. Put in no more than ten pieces at a time and fry, turning, for 3–4 minutes (photo 4).

Assemble five pineapple cubes and five pieces of cooked fish on each serving dish, and then scatter with the toasted sesame seeds. Sprigs of fresh coriander look very attractive as a garnish (this herb goes extremely well with most fish dishes); otherwise settle for sprigs of parsley.

1 Ask your fishmonger to cut off the monkfish head.

2 The fishmonger will also remove the flesh from the single cartilaginous bone.

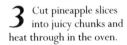

3 Cut pineapple slices into juicy chunks and heat through in the oven.

4 Cut each 4 oz (100 g) portion of fish into five pieces, and fry in the sizzling oil.

AND TO DRINK

The Sauvignon grape would accompany this admirably.

Farmed salmon on French beans with walnut orange dressing

⟡

*S*ALMON IS NO LONGER *a luxury in many households, now that it is being expertly farmed and is available throughout the year. A few years ago I attended a salmon tasting and in no way could I detect a difference in taste or texture between the wild and the farmed.*

It is a very filling dish and although this recipe allows only 2 oz (50 g) per person, even I find this sufficient when *accompanied by new potatoes and a simple green salad. A 1½ lb (700 g) tail of salmon (weight before preparation) will give you enough for six. Photos 1 and 2 show how to bone and skin the salmon.*

Serves 6

78 'matchstick' French beans, weighing about 8–9 oz (225–250 g) before preparation

12 oz (350 g) fresh salmon (boned weight), skinned

4 oz (100 g) softened butter

6 teaspoons ground coriander

6 teaspoons dry white wine

1 To bone the salmon, lay it flat and, using a sharp, serrated knife, cut into the flesh towards the bone in the middle. Remember to put pressure on the knife *away* from you.

2 To skin the two pieces of fish, make a small incision at the tail end just between the skin and flesh. Holding this tail end with your fingers (use a cloth if you wish), cut down on the skin, and the flesh will roll off the knife.

3 Place the circles of salmon on top of the latticed French bean 'gates'.

Dressing

finely grated rind of 2 oranges

2 tablespoons fresh orange juice

5 fl oz (150 ml) walnut oil

1 teaspoon white wine vinegar

1 teaspoon dry English mustard

salt and freshly ground black pepper

Suggested garnishes

sprigs of dill, very finely chopped fennel, lightly cooked asparagus spears, fine strips of lemon, or tiny salads

Pre-heat the oven to gas mark 8, 450°F (230°C).

Top and tail the French beans and part-cook in boiling water for 3 minutes. Drain and leave to soak in cold water to cool. Cut the prepared salmon into small cubes about the size of your thumbnail.

Spread two baking trays with half the butter. On one arrange six portions of 13 French beans each like a five-bar gate with five on the base horizontally and another five on top vertically, and finishing off with the three remaining beans. Leave space between the six portions so that you will be able to transfer them quickly to the dinner plates using a fish slice. Pile the salmon cubes into six rounds on the other baking tray and sprinkle each with a teaspoon (or less) of coriander (this will give a dominant flavour, so use sparingly the first time you try the recipe).

Mix together the dressing ingredients in a saucepan and set to one side.

Just before you put the salmon into the oven pour 1 teaspoon dry white wine over each portion. Cook in the oven for 4 minutes only, putting the French beans in also after 2 minutes. Heat through the saucepan of dressing on top of the stove.

Transfer the French bean arrangements with a fish slice from their baking tray to six warmed plates. Put the salmon circles on top of the beans (photo 3) and pour the heated dressing over the whole lot. Garnish with sprigs of dill if possible. A teaspoon of very finely chopped raw fennel can be scattered on at this stage to give a difference in texture. Lightly cooked spears of fresh asparagus also go well with this dish as a garnish, as does a tiny savoury salad like that in the main picture, composed of scored lemon and cucumber slices, herbs, and a touch of Keta.

AND TO DRINK

Perfect would be a chilled New World Sauvignon Blanc.

Cold sole, spinach and smoked salmon pistachio roll

*O*NCE THE ONLY *cold fish that diners liked and appreciated was salmon with mayonnaise, and this was duly served at Miller Howe from the end of April until mid-June. Of late this dish has been extended until late September, with the delicious wild salmon now marketed so well, mostly by Scottish outlets.*

However, when you are entertaining, and want to serve a fish course, it is sometimes difficult to get your timings right. The following recipe, though, looks very pretty fanned out on the serving plate, and could be dished up mid-afternoon and each portion covered with cling film and left somewhere nice and cool. (Cling film is also used in the cooking, and when I started to use it in this way, certain food critics raised their

eyebrows. But it usually states on the packet whether cling film can be used for cooking, so watch for this when buying.)

The recipe delightfully combines four basic flavours, and your immediate reaction might well be that they would fight one another. But believe you me, the guests who have eaten it all sent back perfectly clean plates and commented favourably on the dish! It can be enhanced by serving a dollop of home-made mayonnaise as well (see p. 166), but I prefer to pour over a little hot *French dressing (see p. 168) just as it is going to the table. The hot walnut oil and orange dressing used with the salmon in the preceding recipe is another which is delicious with this dish. I always serve the fish rolls with a simple dressed green salad and slices of well-buttered wholemeal bread (see p. 162) will make it all go much further.*

I have also enjoyed this dish with the fillet of sole placed first of all on a cold blanched lettuce leaf. I have taken it on picnics and simply placed it inside a well-buttered cob roll! Roughly chopped hazelnuts can be substituted for the pistachios, and thin slices of smoked haddock may be used instead of the smoked salmon.

1 Place the blanched spinach leaf on top of the skinned side of the sole fillet.

2 Lay the salmon strips on top of the spinach-covered sole.

3 Place the rolled sole fillet on a well-buttered square of cling film.

4 Knot the ends of the cling-film 'package' to enclose the sole.

Per person

1 × 6 oz (175 g) sole fillet, skinned

salt and freshly ground black pepper

1 large fresh spinach leaf, stem removed, and blanched (photo 1)

1 × 1 oz (25 g) piece smoked salmon, cut in thin strips

1 teaspoon coarsely chopped pistachio nuts

½ oz (15 g) softened butter

Lay the sole fillet on your work surface flesh-side down, skinned-side up, and season lightly. On top of this place the blanched spinach leaf. On top of this again place the thin strips of smoked salmon (photo 2) with, at one end, the chopped nuts. Starting at this end, roll up the fillet and its contents, and place on a well-buttered square of cling film (photo 3). Roll up in the cling film and then knot the ends as shown in photo 4.

To cook, steam the rolls in a steamer or colander placed over a pan of boiling water (as outlined on p. 56) for 12 minutes. Remove from the steamer and, when cold, take out of the cling film. Slice each roll to your personal liking and then fan out on individual serving plates.

AND TO DRINK

A well-chilled wine made from the Sauvignon grape will enhance the dish.

Salmon, fennel and prawn in wine aspic

*A*LTHOUGH I KNEW *that cold fish dishes went down well with diners, I must admit the kitchen staff weren't at all happy when I decided to serve this 'fish jelly' (even though, after testing, they all agreed that it was delicious). They insisted that the first time it was put on the menu I had to go round the tables in case there were any disgruntled customers. It proved, thankfully, to be a pleasant task, as all the diners commented favourably on the combination of flavours and textures, and, more important still, on how tempting it looked in the Manhattan cocktail glasses! (You don't have to rush out and buy these, by the way, but they are relatively inexpensive and can be used for all kinds of mousses, trifles and other creamy puds, as well as for something like a chilled tomato cocktail with vodka instead of a soup.)*

This is really a dish for making and serving only if you like the wine used for the jelly. There is no such thing as 'cheap' cooking wine, if by 'cheap' you mean something that you wouldn't drink by the glass! It all goes down your throat and into your stomach, so why cook with a certain wine if you wouldn't dream of drinking it? I have no shares or options in any wine company but I do swear by many produced in Australia and New Zealand: they are mostly pure, clean and stylish. Have some fun shopping around your local wine outlets to discover a good New World (or other) Sauvignon Blanc. Some of my favourites are Cloudy Bay, Delegats and Stoneleigh Marlborough from New Zealand, and Cullens from Australia. The Glen Ellen Sauvignon Blanc 1987 from California is also excellent and ideal for this dish.

Fresh salmon these days is no problem to obtain, but prawns can be quite another thing. Use only prawns that you know

are soft and succulent, having first sought out your own favourite and reliable brand. As for the aspic, I prefer to use a brand that is made in Switzerland as it always seems to be superior.

You could serve the dish with a blob of home-made mayonnaise piped on the top of each portion, but I think this detracts from the delicate flavours. What I do serve with it are two very thin slices of wholemeal bread (see p. 162), liberally buttered; just as I am about to serve, I squeeze the merest touch of fresh lemon juice on to each slice.

The dish also looks stunning turned upside down out of the glass, like a pyramid, on to a bed of dressed shredded lettuce.

Serves 4

butter
8 oz (225 g) salmon, skinned and boned
2 tablespoons wine
10 fl oz (300 ml) Sauvignon Blanc wine aspic
4 oz (100 g) prawns (defrosted weight)
4 oz (100 g) bulb fennel, finely chopped
4 teaspoons finely chopped fresh herb fennel or dill

Pre-heat the oven to gas mark 7, 425°F (220°C), and generously butter a lipped baking tray.

Cut the salmon into small cubes and place on the buttered baking tray. Pour over 2 tablespoons wine. Cook in the pre-heated oven for 5 minutes, remove, and then leave until quite cold.

At this stage make up the aspic according to the instructions on the packet and set to one side. Make sure that the prawns are completely defrosted and free of liquid; this can be done by very gently squeezing them in the palm of your hand.

Have your four glasses to hand, and first put in the cold salmon cubes (photo 1), followed by the prawns (photo 2). Add the chopped fennel and herbs (photo 3) then, just as the aspic is beginning to set (this is very important, as aspic should come into contact with food only when it is cold), divide it between the four glasses (photo 4). Place in the fridge to set and chill.

I like to serve each glass on a small plate decorated with a doiley, a fern leaf and a small flower from the garden, offering guests a teaspoon with which to devour the dish.

1 Put the cold salmon cubes into the glass first.

2 Follow them with the prawns.

3 Add the chopped fennel and herbs.

4 Just as the aspic is beginning to set, divide it between the four glasses.

AND TO DRINK

What else but the wine with which you made the aspic?

Roast rib of beef with mini-mustard puddings

O*N CHRISTMAS EVE 1989, restaurateur friends motored* down to the farm from Gullane, near Edinburgh, after serving lunch, and we had our turkey and trimmings for a very late dinner that night. For the mid-afternoon main meal on Christmas day I cooked this rib of beef recipe.

It wasn't any old rib of beef, but one reared with much care in the Rossendale Valley (where I am semi-retired), by a local farmer who slaughters his own stock. Cross-Angus and Charolais are the two breeds he raises, and I have never, ever, had an indifferent joint from him. I know I am lucky as I often shudder with disbelief when I look at many of the joints tightly wrapped in cling film on the brightly lit refrigerated shelves of supermarkets — I often can't even recognise which part of the animal the meat has come from!

I prefer to buy my joint on the bone, and it is best to ask your butcher for the three rib bones nearest the sirloin. Cook the mini-puddings while the meat is resting; you can make the gravy in advance (see p. 180).

Serves 8–12

1 × 7 lb (3 kg) rib joint of beef

softened butter

curry powder

salt

Mini-mustard puddings

4 oz (100 g) strong plain flour

pinch of salt

2 medium eggs, lightly beaten with 5 fl oz (150 ml) cold milk and 3 tablespoons single cream

12 mustard-spoonfuls made English mustard

Pre-heat the oven to the hottest possible temperature. Don't be put off by the amount of fat that coats the meat as this is essential for the cooking. If you don't like it, it can always be removed prior to serving. Trim the top ends of the bones and then lightly smear the joint with butter. Sprinkle it generously with curry powder plus a little salt (photo 1).

Put the joint into the oven, coated fat-side up, and immediately turn the oven down to gas mark 7, 425°F (220°C). Cook for an hour, then lower the temperature to gas mark 6, 400°F (200°C), and cook for a further hour if you want the meat nicely done on the two ends but rare in the middle. (An experienced chef can tell how well a joint of beef has been cooked by simply pressing his fingers into it: if soft and mushy, it is underdone; if soft with a bit of bounce, it is rare; if hard and springy, it is medium; and if fairly firm it is well done.)

Meanwhile, make the mini mustard puddings. Sift the flour and salt into a mixing bowl and make a well in the middle. Into this pour the combined egg, milk and cream mixture and gradually beat the flour in from the sides to make a thickish batter. This can be covered and left until needed, at least an hour.

Remove the joint from the oven, cover it with a double thickness of tinfoil and leave it in a very warm, draught-free place for 20–30 minutes. *Never* carve straight from the oven. Only when the puddings are nearly ready, and it has rested for the requisite time, do you take the meat off the bone to carve as shown in photo 2.

Turn the oven up again to gas mark 7, 425°F (220°C), and, while the meat is resting, cook the mini-mustard puddings. Put a little of the beef dripping in each container of a twelve-hole bun tin (photo 3). Place in the oven to heat through for 10 minutes – the dripping needs to be really boiling.

About 20 minutes before you want to eat, take the bun tin from the oven and pour in your batter. Drop into each portion a mustard-spoonful of mustard (photo 4), place immediately back in the oven and bake for 20 minutes.

1 Sprinkle the joint generously with curry powder and a little salt.

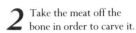

2 Take the meat off the bone in order to carve it.

3 Place a little beef dripping in each container of a bun tin.

4 Drop a spoonful of mustard into each container of batter just before baking.

AND TO DRINK

As for the marinated roast beef fillet with garlic on the next page.

Marinated roast fillet of beef with garlic

FILLET OF BEEF *for me is the most boring of joints, but often over the festive season I get from my local Rossendale butcher a whole sirloin with the full fillet intact. The latter I remove in one whole piece, marinate it for 4–5 days in beer in an airtight container in the fridge, and then plonk the container into the freezer. Believe you me, it has come to my rescue on more than one occasion when I have invited lunch guests to stay on for supper – a spur-of-the-moment idea that seems inspired at the time, but perfectly idiotic when we are finishing the last of the left-over lunch cheese and puds close on midnight!*

You don't have to go through the rigmarole of this if you decide to cook the dish without having enjoyed the sirloin from which the fillet came. Simply give your butcher fair warning of when you will need a well-hung fillet. One weighing 1½ lb (700 g) with the tail end on will give you sufficient, along with veg., etc., for six, and be very generous for four. The marinating will make it lovely and moist throughout when it has been cooked, and adds a titillating flavour. Accompany the roast fillet with hollandaise sauce, which takes the dish into a class of its own, and onion marmalade, which will be a source of considerable and favourable comment (make this well in advance, and warm through gently before serving). To stretch the dish even further, make some accompanying rösti potatoes (see p. 100); they'll take only about 5 minutes!

Serves 4–6

1 × 1½ lb (700 g) beef fillet
1 pint (600 ml) beer of your choice (I usually use an Export type: Guinness or stout dominate the dish somewhat!)
3 fresh, plump garlic cloves, peeled
6 oz (175 g) beef dripping
sea salt and freshly ground black pepper

Make sure that all the skin is removed from the fillet, and simply marinate the meat in the beer for at least 4 days in a covered dish in the fridge (photo 1). Remove from the marinade on the day you plan to serve it.

The fillet is thick at one end and then tails away at the other. To start with, you have to bring this tail piece back over sufficiently to make the whole piece quite even and round like a Swiss roll. Do this and tie firmly in place. Dry well on kitchen paper.

Have ready a heavy-based flameproof dish or small roasting tin in which the fillet and the beef dripping will fit snugly. Pre-heat the oven to gas mark 8, 450°F (230°C), or as high as it will go.

Cut the garlic into slivers and, after making small incisions in the fillet at even intervals, insert these slivers quite firmly (photo 2). Melt the dripping in the

1 Marinate the beef fillet in the beer for at least 4 days.

2 Insert the slivers of garlic into incisions in the fillet.

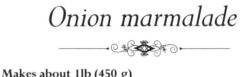

3 Before roasting, seal the fillet on all sides, so that it is well browned.

4 Slice the meat very thinly on a slight angle.

flameproof dish or tin on top of the stove, and allow it to start sizzling. (It should be as hot as possible.) Coat the prepared fillet generously with sea salt and freshly ground black pepper and seal in the sizzling fat. This takes only minutes, but make sure that you turn it to seal it on all sides and brown it well (photo 3).

Put the browned meat immediately into the pre-heated oven and cook for 20 minutes, basting every 5 minutes, and turning over in the fat. Remove from the oven and take the meat out of the dish or tin. Leave for 5 minutes if you intend to serve it hot; however you serve it, carve it very thinly on the diagonal to give larger-looking pieces (photo 4). Serve with hollandaise sauce, onion marmalade and rösti potatoes (see p. 100).

Hollandaise sauce

THIS CAN EASILY be made in a liquidiser or, better still, in a blender.

Serves 6

3 egg yolks

pinch of salt

1 teaspoon caster sugar

1 tablespoon each white wine vinegar and lemon juice

6 oz (75 g) butter

Put the egg yolks, salt and sugar into a liquidiser or blender and blend. Heat the wine vinegar and lemon juice together in a pan until sizzling and, with the machine running at full speed, *slowly* dribble into the egg mixture. Melt the butter in another small pan to

bubbling point, and once again *slowly* dribble this into the machine. If you rush it, your sauce will be quite thin, and will thicken only as it cools. Serve warm with the beef.

Onion marmalade

Makes about 1 lb (450 g)

6 tablespoons good-quality olive oil

2 lb (900 g) onions, peeled and finely sliced

6 tablespoons demerara sugar

4 tablespoons sherry vinegar

Heat the oil in a large saucepan, add the sliced onions and mix in the sugar. Over a medium heat cook for about 2 hours, stirring from time to time to ensure that the onions don't stick – you will be surprised at how much they fall. Add the vinegar, stir well and then continue to cook for 30–45 minutes until you get the gooey mess you want!

AND TO DRINK

With the beef I would serve a wine made from my favourite Merlot grape. Or you could serve your own favourite claret – not necessarily one from the upper end of the market, but one of those from the excellent multiple wine stores in the high street.

Leg of old lamb baked in hay with herbs

L AST WINTER WHEN the staff and I visited the US — to dispel the myth about English food consisting of overcooked beef with soggy cabbage — leg of lamb baked in hay with herbs was the main course each evening.

We travelled with five trunks loaded with fresh yeast, English flour and a couple of sacks of Lakeland hay! Every single night, when the kitchen brigade and I came out after the meal to urge the diners to visit the UK, somebody would ask: 'Where did the hay come from?' And this was followed by: 'What if there was something in it?' — to which I always replied: 'If there was, it wouldn't survive cooking at that high temperature for 2½ hours!'

No doubt you have been making your own mint sauce for ages — but for a change try adding a little dry English mustard to your mix and then fold in a small apple that has been peeled, cored, thinly sliced and then cut up into tiny cubes.

Serves 8–12

6 lb (2.75 kg) leg of old lamb, trimmed

8 garlic cloves, peeled

2 sprigs of rosemary, cut into 8 small pieces

1 oz (25 g) softened butter

2 tablespoons finely chopped fresh herbs

sea salt and freshly ground black pepper

5 fl oz (150 ml) red cooking wine or water (for the puritanical)

6 oz (175 g) clean hay (your local pet shop should oblige)

Pre-heat the oven to gas mark 8, 450°F (230°C), and have ready a roasting tin which will hold the whole leg of lamb, including the knuckle bone — it will need to be approximately 12 × 16 in (30 × 40 cm).

Wipe the lamb with a dry cloth and lay it skin-side up on a work surface. Using a small, sharp, pointed knife, make eight incisions in the flesh, leaving equal

1 Tuck whole peeled garlic cloves into incisions in the leg of lamb.

2 Lay the buttered, seasoned and herbed lamb in a roasting tin lined with foil and hay, and cover with more hay.

3 Hold the leg bone end in a cloth, or with a glove, and carve the meat at a 45-degree angle . . .

4 . . . or carve it horizontally, following the middle bone.

distances between each, and into these place the garlic cloves (photo 1). Force in a piece of rosemary alongside each clove. Spread the butter all over this surface, then scatter the chopped herbs on top and be liberal with the sea salt and black pepper.

Line the roasting tin with tinfoil – the sides as well as the base – and put half the hay on the base. Lay the prepared leg on this and cover with the remaining hay (photo 2). Pour over the wine or water and then completely cover, with another large piece of tinfoil. Put into the pre-heated oven and do not attempt to look at the leg for 2½ hours – have faith, please, reader!

At the end of the cooking time remove from the oven and carefully take off the top layer of foil and keep to one side. Take the leg out of the roasting tin and discard all the hay. Return the leg to the tin, cover with the reserved foil and leave to rest in a warm place for 10 minutes before you start to carve.

Personally I prefer to carve the leg as shown in photo 3. I use the leg bone end as an anchor in my non-carving hand and then slice at a 45-degree angle towards the knuckle, immediately putting the meat on to warmed dinner plates or a serving platter. However, I have discovered a way to carve which can be done 20 minutes before serving and which looks quite clever when you serve the meat to your guests. In photo 4 you will see that the leg is held in exactly the same way but you carve *horizontally*, following the middle bone. As each slice comes off, place on top of it each successive slice and, when down to the bone, build the joint back up again. Wrap the whole thing in a double thickness of foil and keep in a warm oven for 20 minutes. It's an easy task then to dish the meat out!

AND TO DRINK

I would recommend a Nobilos Cabernet Sauvignon from New Zealand.

Lamb chops with pineapple and ginger

*T*HIS IS A CASSEROLE *that I like to serve when friends come round for a meal at my farmhouse. It can be prepared way ahead of time; and indeed it will come to no harm if frozen. In fact, I usually make a point of doubling up on the quantities that I need for immediate use and I freeze half, tied in individual plastic bags.*

New-season lamb is no good for this dish — you really want a beast bordering on good old-fashioned mutton, at least a year old but preferably two. It is such a pity that many high-street butchers fight shy of advertising that it is actually mutton they are selling because of the fashion for young lamb. You therefore have to use your common sense when shopping for it: look for good, thick, fatty cutlets with dark skin.

The most important stage in this recipe is the initial cooking of the prepared cutlets — they must sing, sizzle and seal, not sweat, simmer and steam. I like to use two 7 in (18 cm) frying-pans for this 'frying off' process and, although this adds time to the preparation, the final dish is better for the care. However, if you have only one larger pan, never seal more than two cutlets at a time.

Use a pair of tongs to turn the cutlets over, or two wooden spoons. Never stab a fork into the flesh to turn them — this just allows the escape of the juices that you have taken time frying to keep in!

Serves 6

12 lamb cutlets, weighing just over 4 oz (100 g) each when trimmed

lightly seasoned flour

4 tablespoons olive oil

4 oz (100 g) butter

12 circles of tinned pineapple with juice

6 'nuts' of preserved ginger, finely chopped

Optional garnish

watercress

1 Gently heat half the oil and butter together in a frying-pan before frying the cutlets.

2 When the fat is 'singing', sear and seal the seasoned cutlets, two at a time, on both sides.

3 Don't forget to seal the fat edge and the exposed meaty end of each cutlet.

4 Transfer the sealed cutlets to doubled kitchen paper to drain while you seal the remainder.

Pre-heat the oven to gas mark 2, 300°F (150°C).

Dry the trimmed cutlets on kitchen paper and coat lightly with seasoned flour. Warm half the olive oil in a frying-pan and add half the butter to melt slowly and gently (photo 1).

Turn up the heat and, when it starts to 'sing', immediately place two cutlets flat-side down in the pan (photo 2). Turn each cutlet over, seal the fatty edge (photo 3) and also the exposed meaty end. Transfer to a double thickness of kitchen paper (photo 4).

Fry the rest of the cutlets in the same way, adding more oil and butter half-way through. Remember to listen again for the sizzle before continuing to seal the cutlets.

Open the tins of pineapple and reserve six of the rings and the juice. Coarsely chop the remaining rings. Lay the sealed cutlets in an ovenproof dish, cover with chopped pineapple, chopped ginger and pineapple juice, then cover with tinfoil. Bake in the pre-heated oven for 2 hours. At this stage the dish can be removed from the oven, cooled and frozen. Otherwise take off the tinfoil, turn up the oven to gas mark 4, 350°F (180°C), and cook for a further 30 minutes.

Place the reserved pineapple rings on a buttered baking tray and cook in the oven for the final 15 minutes of the total time. When serving, garnish the rings with watercress or lay them on the serving plate with two cutlets per person placed on top.

AND TO DRINK

I would look for a relatively inexpensive red made from the Pinot Noir grape, served slightly chilled, or perhaps a dry Cabernet Sauvignon.

Bobotie

I HAVE BEEN VISITING *southern Africa for more years than I actually care to remember. I first went as a junior cadet officer in the Colonial Service way back in 1949, sailing on the* Winchester Castle. *I enjoyed every moment of the voyage, as there was food in abundance for once – the most memorable aspect of escape from rationed Britain. Nobody ever forgets their first sighting of the majestic Table Mountain, but what sticks in my mind still was the warm welcome of the people. The same applies even now, and my adrenalin always starts flowing as the plane flies over the Stellenbosch Mountains.*

Bobotie is a Cape Malay dish normally made from Karoo lamb and, as with Lancashire hotpot and so many other dishes

throughout the world, each household has its own version. Bobotie often used to feature on the lunch menu of South African Railways on the 3-day journey from Cape Town to Rhodesia.

Serves 6–8

4 oz (100 g) dried apricots, soaked overnight in 4 tablespoons cooking brandy or sherry

2 oz (50 g) mutton fat or butter

6 oz (175 g) onions, peeled and finely chopped

2 juicy garlic cloves, peeled and crushed with 1 teaspoon free-running salt

2 lb (900 g) shoulder of lamb, minced

salt and freshly ground black pepper

2 tablespoons tomato purée

curry essence to taste (see p. 170) or 1 tablespoon curry powder

2 oz (50 g) nibbed almonds, toasted

Custard topping

10 fl oz (300 ml) double cream

2 eggs plus 1 egg yolk

own essence, introduce it little by little half-way through the cooking to achieve the flavour you want. Don't forget that you still have to add the sweet apricots.

When the lamb has cooked for 30 minutes, fold in the apricots and almonds and turn the mixture into a 3 pint (1.75 litre) ovenproof dish approximately 9 in (23 cm) in diameter. Mix the custard topping ingredients together and pour over the lamb (photo 2). Put the dish in a bain-marie filled with hot water (photo 3) and bake in the pre-heated oven for 35 minutes.

Remove from the oven and leave for 5 minutes before serving.

1 Mix the seasoned lamb with the onions and garlic and cook for 30 minutes.

2 Turn the meat mixture into a dish and top with the creamy custard.

3 Place the dish in a bain-marie of hot water for the final cooking.

4 To accompany the bobotie, stir-fry blanched, grated root vegetables until brown.

Stir-fried grated root vegetables

THE BASIC BOBOTIE recipe is delicious served with pasta, or used as a filling for pasties or pancakes, but it is also good served with the following.

1 lb (450 g) assorted root vegetables, coarsely grated

2 tablespoons olive oil

2 oz (50 g) softened butter

Mix the grated vegetables together in a bowl, cover with boiling water, leave for 1 minute, then drain and pat dry on kitchen paper. When you are ready to serve the bobotie, heat the oil and butter in a frying-pan and stir-fry the vegetables for 3-4 minutes or until brown (photo 4), adding seasoning to taste.

Pre-heat the oven to gas mark 5, 375°F (190°C).

Drain the apricots, reserving the alcohol, and chop them coarsely or mince them. Melt the fat in a large frying-pan and cook the onions and garlic over a medium heat until just golden: do not burn them.

Season the lamb well and mix in the tomato purée and reserved alcohol. Add to the onions (photo 1) and cook for 30 minutes over a medium heat, stirring from time to time. If you are using curry powder, add this at the start of the cooking time; if you have made your

AND TO DRINK

Serve a gutsy South African red with your bobotie.

Watercress-stuffed loin of pork with apple sauce

*A*T ONE TIME, *our family would have a roast leg of pork on the last Sunday in April, and then pork would not be seen again in the household until the first Sunday in September. The belief that one should never eat pork when there wasn't an 'r' in the month was strictly adhered to; now pork is sold, bought, cooked and served all year round. That leg, being a large joint, was served cold in thin slices with pan-fried chips on wash-day Monday, cold with hot veg. and baked potatoes on Tuesday, used as the basis of a made-up dish for Wednesday, and then the remnants finally used in pasties or stuffed cabbage on Thursday!*

When you are able to get good pork from a decent butcher, simply roasting it takes a lot of beating. Up here in the Lakes we are blessed with a splendid supplier and I am able, right through the season, to serve this dish with a lovely ¼ in (5 mm) thick piece of superb crackling. Best-quality pork is pale pink in colour with pure white fat and a smooth rind. To make crackling, some people flour the skin or rub oil and salt into it so that it will roast crisp, or even — heaven forbid! — remove the skin and cook it separately under the grill. The only infallible way of getting a crisp, toffee-like finish is to find a supplier who has never blast-chilled his meat but simply kept the loin or leg hanging in a refrigerated cold room for at least 2 weeks.

The meat you want for this dish should come from a fairly young animal, as older joints are normally used for smoking. Ask your kind butcher to chop most of the way through· the thick bone end, and to score the rind for you.

Serves 4

2½ lb (1.1 kg) loin of pork on the bone (about 4 thickish chops), with rind

soft sea salt

Stuffing

2 oz (50 g) butter

4 oz (100 g) onions, peeled and finely chopped

4 oz (100 g) ground hazelnuts

1 bunch of fresh watercress, washed and finely chopped

salt and freshly ground black pepper

Creamy apple sauce

4 apples (preferably Granny Smith)

a little sugar according to taste and the variety of apple

generous knob of butter

4 tablespoons double cream

a little chopped fresh mint, sage or rosemary, according to taste

If your pork rind has not been scored, the best knife to use is a Stanley knife with its razor-sharp small blade and firm small handle (photo 1). Then, to make a hole in the meat for the stuffing, push a long, sharp-ended knife through the middle of the fleshy part of the joint from each end towards the middle (photo 2). Standing the joint on one end, waggle either a steel or the handle of a wooden spoon about in this incision to make it larger (photo 3).

To prepare the stuffing, melt the butter in a frying-pan and cook the chopped onions until golden. Fold in the ground hazelnuts, chopped watercress and some salt and pepper, and leave to cool. When the stuffing is quite cold, place it in a piping bag without a nozzle, and pipe from each end of the joint into the middle of the hole in the flesh (photo 4). This can, of course, all be done the day before – simply cover the prepared joint with cling film and keep it in the fridge until you are ready to cook.

Pre-heat the oven to gas mark 8, 450°F (230°C). Just prior to cooking, dip your clean hand in cold water and rub this on to the pork rind, then sprinkle generously with soft sea salt. Place the joint in a roasting tin, rind uppermost, and put it in the oven. It will be ready in 45 minutes.

Meanwhile, make the apple sauce. Simply peel, core and thinly slice the apples and put into a saucepan with a fairly thick base. Add the sugar and butter and simmer over a medium heat until the apples fall and

become quite mushy. Liquidise with the double cream and herbs and the sauce is ready. This too can be made ahead of time and simply warmed through again in a bowl over a pan of simmering water.

Take the roast out of the oven and allow it to rest, covered with a clean cloth, in a warm place for about 10 minutes. Using a large carving knife, separate the four chops. Alternatively, take the loin off the bone and carve into thin slices, garnishing with the strips of crackling.

When serving, put the apple sauce on the warmed dinner plates first and lay the chops or slices of pork on top of it. You get a delightful effect which shows off the stuffing to great advantage.

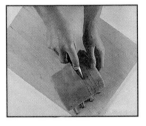

1 A Stanley knife is the best one to use for scoring pork rind.

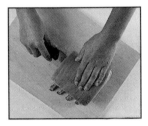

2 To make a hole in the joint for the stuffing, push a long, sharp-ended knife into the middle of the meaty part from both ends.

3 Waggle the handle of a wooden spoon or steel in the hole to make it larger.

4 Pipe the cold stuffing into the hole in the meat from both ends.

AND TO DRINK

A Sauvignon grape is a **must***, and one of those from the southern hemisphere would hold its own beautifully with this dish.*

Barbecued meat and kebabs

*B*ARBECUES CAN BE FRAUGHT *or fun: fraught if you start with indifferent dips into which raw vegetable chunks are to be dunked, endless bags of commercial crisps, olives and fancy savoury biscuits, followed by undercooked chunks of chicken or burnt-to-a-cinder cubes of unrecognisable meats; fun, on the other hand, if a little thought and planning are put into the occasion.*

No matter what sort of barbecue equipment you use, it is essential to have the correct fuel and to light it properly at the outset. I roll up double sheets of old newspapers into long strips and then roll each of these like a Catherine wheel, tucking the end bit through the tight middle. I lay them on the barbecue base quite liberally and then spread thin splints of dry tomato or orange boxes over them. On top of this I spread charcoal cubes (slightly more expensive but much quicker and cleaner to use). I must admit that I am invariably impatient and find myself squirting on some of the non-smelling lighting fuel that is available these days. It takes at least 40 minutes for the coals to become lovely and white: then, and only then, can you start the actual cooking process.

1 Chunks of various fruit and vegetables go well with meats in kebabs.

2 'Stitch' a long strip of bacon between each chunk.

3 The finished kebab can be as elaborate or simple as you like.

4 Ease the kebab off the skewer and on to a plate using a strong kitchen fork.

MARINATING MEAT

However, it is the marinating that will make for pieces of meat with lovely, crisp, barbecued outsides and delicious, juicy insides! You should marinate each type of meat in a separate air-tight container, and keep them in the fridge for 4–5 days if possible. Twice a day take each box out and carefully turn the meats in the marinade before returning to the fridge. Cook the meats liberally coated with marinade and during the cooking baste frequently.

The following are suggested marinades for various types of meat. Adjust the quantities to suit your needs, and combine the ingredients well before using them.

FOR BEEF STEAKS OR CUBES ───────────
Use 2 fat, juicy garlic cloves, peeled and pressed to a paste using a sharp knife – not a garlic press – with ½ teaspoon runny salt, 4 tablespoons each of red cooking wine, bottled tomato sauce and olive oil, 1 tablespoon each of wine vinegar and Worcestershire sauce and 1 teaspoon soft brown sugar. Use lots of freshly ground black pepper during the actual cooking.

FOR LAMB CHOPS OR CUBES ───────────
Shoulder is best for the latter. Mix 2 crushed garlic cloves as above with 4 tablespoons each of fresh lemon juice, dry white wine and olive oil, and a few sprigs of fresh garden mint. Use lots of freshly ground coriander during cooking.

FOR CHICKEN BREASTS, DRUMSTICKS OR CUBES ───────────
You need lashings of natural yoghurt and the rind and juice of a fresh lime. Use a little curry powder during cooking. Keep skin on breasts and drumsticks.

FOR PORK CHOPS OR CUBES ───────────
Remove skin. I recommend simply coconut milk, and that you sprinkle on a little paprika during cooking.

KEBABS

Kebabs can reduce the cost of a barbecue as well as adding interest, if you use a variety of ingredients, not just chunks of meat, marinated as above.

In photo 1, besides marinated cubes of pork, there are pineapple cubes, mushroom caps, onion chunks, red pepper pieces, water chestnuts, sage leaves and long strips of bacon. All of these extras go quite well with any of the listed meats.

Photo 2 shows a kebab being started off (on a rather posh skewer made in Morocco, but wooden skewers can be bought from Oriental shops and do the job just as well, provided they are well soaked in water beforehand). The end bit of a thin bacon rasher sits next to a cube of meat, and the bacon is skewered again before the next item is added.

Photo 3 shows a finished skewer, with the bacon looking like a big dipper going up and down between each piece of food. You can put two or three portions on a long skewer.

Taking cooked meat off the skewer is easy with a strong kitchen fork. Push this on to the skewer at the handle end, and ease the kebab off (photo 4).

AND TO DRINK

Depending on the meat you've barbecued, I would recommend a robust Shiraz grape served slightly chilled.

Basic mince

━━━━━━ ◦◦◦✦◦◦◦ ━━━━━━

*Y*OU MAY THINK MINCE *is boring, but done my way it is anything but! There are innumerable uses for a basic — or tarted-up — mince, and to have some ready, either fresh or in the freezer, can be very handy, particularly between Christmas and New Year when, fed up with a constant diet of turkey, and tired of the other numerous goodies you have devoured, you are longing for something more down to earth.*

Serves 4–6, depending on usage

1 tablespoon olive oil

1 oz (25 g) softened butter

4 oz (100 g) onions, peeled and finely chopped

2 garlic cloves, peeled and crushed to a paste with 1 teaspoon salt

1 tablespoon tomato purée

1 lb (450 g) minced meat

In your frying-pan gently heat the olive oil, melt the butter with it and, when hot, cook the chopped onions until golden. Add the garlic paste, stir in the tomato purée and the mince and cook, uncovered, for 15–20 minutes or until the meat is browned.

The following are flavouring variations for savoury minced beef, pork and lamb. These should be added to the mixture at the same time as the garlic paste.

SAVOURY MINCED BEEF

1 tablespoon Worcestershire sauce

1 tablespoon chutney of your taste

2 tablespoons chopped fresh or 1 tablespoon dried parsley

SAVOURY MINCED PORK

1 tablespoon soy sauce

2 tablespoons desiccated coconut

2 tablespoons chopped fresh or 1 tablespoon dried mint

1 Line the loaf tin with bacon, leaving the thinner ends of the rashers overhanging.

2 Fill the bacon-lined tin with mince and fold over the bacon ends to cover the top.

3 Place the tin in a bain-marie of boiling water and put it into the oven to cook.

SAVOURY MINCED LAMB

1 tablespoon freshly ground coriander seeds

2 tablespoons apricot jam

1 tablespoon nibbed almonds

curry powder or paste to taste

The minces can be served with cooked macaroni (main picture, top left corner, with cheesy coating) or other pasta; with easily cooked rice; in the middle of a circle of lovely buttery, well-mashed potatoes with a hint of freshly ground nutmeg; or used to make the bottom and top layer of the potato flan on p. 104.

Baked potatoes can be cut in half and topped with mince. Pancakes can be stuffed with it, and, if you want to re-heat them, place on well buttered baking trays and cover with a double thickness of dampened greaseproof paper. The pancakes take only 20 minutes to heat through at gas mark 4, 350°F (180°C); you can then top them with grated cheese and 'flash' under a hot grill.

Put mince on the base of six individual 3 in (7.5 cm) ramekins, then top with potatoes or flavoured egg custard – 10 fl oz (300 ml) double cream to 2 eggs and 1 egg yolk beaten up with a pinch of nutmeg. These will cook in 30 minutes in a bain-marie in the oven at gas mark 5, 375°F (190°C). A 1 lb (450 g) loaf tin may be lined with 10 oz (275 g) smoked bacon (photo 1) and then filled with raw seasoned minced meat of your choice bound together with a lightly beaten egg (photo 2). Cooked in the oven for 45 minutes in a bain-marie (photo 3), this will give you a tasty meat loaf (main picture) for salads or sandwiches.

The minces can form the basis of cottage pie – try adding 4 oz (100 g) finely diced assorted root vegetables as well. They are also useful for moussaka: top with 5 fl oz (150 ml) double cream heated through and reduced by half with 4 oz (100 g) finely shredded firm stale cheese (or the outer rim of Stilton) beaten in and melted. This topping is also delicious with mince and pasta (see main picture). It goes without saying that you can ring the changes with any fresh herbs and your own favourite spices.

AND TO DRINK

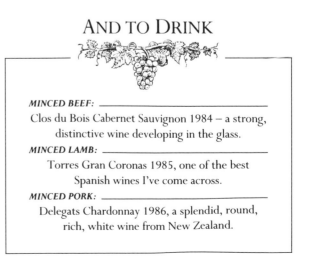

MINCED BEEF:
Clos du Bois Cabernet Sauvignon 1984 – a strong, distinctive wine developing in the glass.

MINCED LAMB:
Torres Gran Coronas 1985, one of the best Spanish wines I've come across.

MINCED PORK:
Delegats Chardonnay 1986, a splendid, round, rich, white wine from New Zealand.

Breast of chicken with barbecue sauce

*R*ECENTLY WE WERE ASKED to cook an English dinner in the States, and my submission of this dish as the main course actually lost us the contract! In my opinion it was their loss. Chickens are not very popular now in the US, because most of those sold in the supermarkets there bear no resemblance to the delicious, plump, free-range birds I am used to. These are becoming more readily available in the UK as people grow more discerning in their shopping.

Your immediate reaction could well be that it is wasteful to buy a whole chicken and use only the breasts to feed two people. You don't – the legs are easily removed and used separately. Just cut them again, dividing the thigh and drumstick, coat lavishly with yoghurt and marinate in an air-tight container in the fridge for up to 5 days. They can then be baked for 40 minutes and are juicy, tender and delicious. You could, of course, buy just the breasts, which must come still attached to the ribcage. Remember there's always more flavour to chicken cooked on the bone.

Serve the chicken hot with vegetables and, as in the main picture, some tomato and mustard cream sauce (see p. 164). Alternatively, allow it to cool, slice it very thinly and serve on a tossed green salad containing finely sliced radishes or even a little freshly grated horseradish. At the last moment add a tablespoon of your own favourite home-made French dressing (see p. 168), but this time heat it before putting it on to the cold chicken and salad (see also p. 90).

Another way of serving the chicken cold, after halving and removing from the bone, is to cut it into fairly thick wedges and garnish it with orange segments (see p. 15) and sprigs of parsley, secured with cocktail sticks, to make substantial cocktail snacks.

Serves 2

1 fresh chicken, legs removed

4 oz (100 g) cheese and herb pâté (see p. 16)

Barbecue sauce

2 tablespoons olive oil

1 tablespoon tomato purée

1 dessertspoon Worcestershire sauce

1 teaspoon soy sauce

1 teaspoon soft brown sugar

generous pinch of ground ginger (optional)

Ease the soft cheese and herb pâté between the skin and the flesh of the chicken breast by using the tips of your fingers (photo 1). Be careful not to break the skin. Wrap the chicken in cling film and refrigerate. This will set the pâté while you get on with other tasks.

Whisk together the barbecue sauce ingredients and set aside: this can also be done ahead of time, if you wish.

When you want to cook, pre-heat the oven to gas mark 5, 375°F (190°C), and remove the cling film from the chicken. Baste the chicken with the barbecue sauce, then put it in the oven and cook for 40 minutes, basting once or twice during this time (photo 2). The chicken will come out of the oven with a rather black look, but the barbecued taste and the lovely crisp skin are absolutely mouth-watering (photo 3).

I simply use a large cleaver type knife to portion the breast into two (photo 4). A suggestion for less nimble hands is that a pair of thick but pliable rubber gloves should be used to protect them while cutting. The breasts will stay crisp for 20 minutes if tightly wrapped in tinfoil and left in the oven at gas mark 1, 275°F (140°C).

The most important thing is not to be put off by the apparently burned, dry look; and if you do serve it to guests and you catch them looking aghast, just turn on the charm!

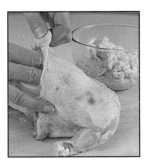

1 Carefully ease the soft pâté between the flesh and skin of the chicken breast.

2 Baste the chicken with barbecue sauce before putting it in the oven – and several times during cooking.

3 Don't worry – the chicken *should* be black and crisp when it comes out of the oven!

4 Use a large cleaver-type knife to cut down the breastbone and divide the chicken in two.

AND TO DRINK

Without any doubt a buttery Chardonnay is the ideal wine for this. Most of the large wine stores now proudly display and sell the better ones from Australia and New Zealand.

Breast of chicken with peanut butter and cornflakes

PEANUTS IN ALL SHAPES and forms were very much part of my culinary background when I worked in Central Africa in the early fifties. I am sure many of you will recall the farce of the nationally proclaimed groundnut scheme which was going to bring prosperity to those of the bush interior of Tanganyika, and help the West with its acute shortage of oils after the war. What I remember, though, are seemingly miles and miles of cultivated bundu literally barren, rusted tractors in profusion, complicated farm equipment which no locals understood or could work, and a general air of despair amongst the local populace, totally bewildered by what was going on. It was my first experience of bureaucratic bungling!

The peanut, or groundnut, actually originates from Brazil, but is now the staple diet of millions in Africa and the Far East, made into soups, stews and stuffings. Its long, oily seed produces both oil and butter, the latter made simply by emulsifying the oil with the nuts. I always keep a jar of peanut butter in my fridge and it is there for the occasional midnight raid when I am tense and under stress. I creep to the kitchen, take out the jar and dig in with my fingers knowing that it isn't doing me the slightest bit of good, but enjoying every mouthful!

Recently, when I had a family staying with me from New York, peanut butter saved me from an embarrassing situation. The little boy's vocabulary consisted basically of 'no' as far as I was concerned. 'Would you like some lunch?' 'Neow.' 'Would you like some tea?' 'Neow.' And so it went on. As soon as I escaped, his mother would make him peanut butter and blackcurrant jelly sandwiches, and he was as happy as a gutso in a gourmet shop. I decided that I wouldn't let him get the better of me, so I started to use peanut butter in my cooking for the family. Before he left the little boy was actually eating the dish reproduced here together with a cream sauce (see p. 164) flavoured with some commercial tomato chutney. Not long afterwards I put the chicken on the menu at Miller Howe, served on a very rich spiced tomato sauce and topped with a

spoonful of Cumberland sauce. Lovely creamed potatoes made smooth with olive oil and garlic paste wouldn't go amiss either!

For two portions, you need to buy one full chicken breast (or supreme) on the ribcage (the two sides), or two breasts already divided, or you can buy a whole fresh chicken, cut the breasts off and use the legs for another dish.

1 Stand the ribcage of the chicken on the wings and pull the skin off carefully.

Serves 2

1 full supreme of chicken on the bone
4 tablespoons natural yoghurt
2 tablespoons peanut butter (crunchy or smooth)
1 oz (25 g) cornflakes, coarsely crushed
butter for greasing

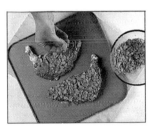

2 Gently ease the flesh away from the ribcage using a small, sharp, pointed knife.

Stand the chicken ribcage on its wings and pull the skin off carefully (photo 1). Using a small, sharp, pointed knife, start cutting through the middle of the flesh towards you, gently feeling for the bone and easing the flesh away from the ribcage (photo 2). Take your time and do not panic.

Marinate the breasts for at least 24 hours in the yoghurt, and then liberally coat with the peanut butter (photo 3). Coat thereafter, equally liberally, with the crushed cornflakes (photo 4). At this stage the breasts can be encased in cling film and left until you wish to cook them.

3 After yoghurt marination, coat the chicken breasts liberally with peanut butter.

Pre-heat the oven to gas mark 4, 350°F (180°C), and paint a baking tray generously with soft butter Remove cling film, place the coated chicken breasts on the tray and put into the pre-heated oven to cook for 30 minutes. Use a fish slice to transfer to warmed plates

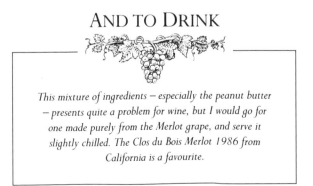

4 Then coat them as generously with crushed cornflakes.

AND TO DRINK

This mixture of ingredients — especially the peanut butter — presents quite a problem for wine, but I would go for one made purely from the Merlot grape, and serve it slightly chilled. The Clos du Bois Merlot 1986 from California is a favourite.

Cold sliced breast of chicken on salad with mustard dressing

I LOVE NOTHING MORE *on my days off than to have guests over at the farm for dinner or to stay overnight. The sheer anticipation is, for me, as happy as the actual time spent planning the meal course by course, doing the shopping, standing in the kitchen preparing the food, laying the table, knowing exactly what will be served on each plate and, more important still, where the dirty dishes will be neatly stacked so that at the end of the evening the kitchen doesn't resemble a battlefield. (I wonder if you are like me and change the menu three times before you finalise your plan of campaign?)*

It is not an easy task being the sole master of ceremonies, as I am these days, but I have got home entertaining down to a fine art, as I invariably serve a hot starter, cold main course and then a warm pudding. Even in the midst of winter I have had no complaints as the conservatory (which is where we eat) is lovely and warm, and it means I can go overboard on the first course and have the main course arranged and covered with cling film way ahead of time. In winter the pud is usually the sticky toffee pudding on p. 134, and the summer sees me serving a choice of two different farmhouse pies.

Fortunately most major supermarkets these days sell smallish packets of assorted new lettuce leaves — iceberg, oakleaf, radicchio, curly endive and so on — and these are a must *for this dish. I still find that the best way to prepare the leaves is to submerge them in a clean sink of cold water, lightly tossing them in the water with both hands. I then use one of those plastic 'spin-driers' to dry them perfectly.*

Each individual main-course plate is first rubbed well with a peeled and crushed clove of garlic. The various lettuce leaves are attractively laid out on the plate. Each plate then requires 13 topped and tailed Kenya French beans that have been steamed for 4 minutes, coated with a trickle of walnut or hazelnut oil, and left to go cold. These are made into a 'five-bar gate' (see p. 64). Scatter over this toasted cashew nuts (at least 12 per person), very thin slices of fresh, firm celery, and about 1 tablespoon finely chopped red pepper. Finish off the mound with sprigs or leaves of any fresh herbs you have to hand or that are to your personal taste.

Steam the chicken breasts for 10 minutes (as described on p. 57) and leave to cool completely. Slice them as thinly as possible and arrange, overlapping, on top of the basic salad creation. At this stage the plates may be covered with cling film and left somewhere quite cold until needed: as there is no dressing on the salad (apart from the mere trickle of oil used on the French beans), it will come to no harm.

The runny mustard dressing is then poured over the chicken just as it goes to the table. Be generous with this because, as you cut into the salad underneath, you want it to run through to moisten the lettuce leaves. Garnish each plate with sprigs of fresh watercress; if you are lucky enough to have borage flowers, a couple of these will set the dish off magnificently. Serve with thick, well-buttered slices of brown yoghurt seed loaf (p. 163).

Mustard dressing

2 medium eggs

½ teaspoon free-running salt

½ teaspoon caster sugar

2 teaspoons fresh lemon juice

1 tablespoon dry English mustard

1 tablespoon white wine vinegar

10 fl oz (300 ml) good-quality olive oil or 5 fl oz (150 ml) olive oil and 5 fl oz (150 ml) white wine

Put all the ingredients except the olive oil into your liquidiser or food processor and blend. Dribble the oil in quite slowly while the machine is going.

Those folk who might find an oil dressing not to their liking could use half-oil and half-white wine, but the result will be much runnier.

AND TO DRINK

*To combat the mustard, I would serve something fruity —
a Gewürztraminer perhaps.*

Roast duck

*N*OBODY *IN MY OPINION used to cook duck quite like Mrs Johnson and her daughter-in-law, Barbara, at Tully-thwaite House, in the Lythe Valley. The skin was as crisp as a toffee apple and the succulent meat fell off the shrivelled bones: none of your sickly and silly* nouvelle cuisine, *with the flesh oozing blood and playing havoc with your false teeth! They always insisted that an Aga was the secret of their success.*

Years and hundreds of ducks later I have to disagree. The most important factor is simply that fresh *duck must always, but always, be used, and this will give you the good old-fashioned flavour and texture.*

Serves 4

1 fresh, plump duck, weighing at least 3¹/₄ lb (1.4 kg)

1 carrot, scrubbed and trimmed

1 small onion, peeled and quartered

1 large parsley sprig

sea salt and freshly ground black pepper

Garnish

4 orange wedges

4 glacé cherries

4 parsley sprigs

Pre-heat the oven to gas mark 9, 475°F (240°C) – or as hot as possible; some new ovens are graded only to gas mark 8, 450°F (230°C), in which case an extra 15 minutes' cooking time is necessary. Have to hand two very thick, heat-resistant gloves and a warmed Pyrex bowl in which to collect the duck fat (which has endless uses).

I prefer to time my meal so that the main course is served immediately the bird is portioned, straight from the oven. Better the guests wait an extra 10 minutes than that the cooked duck waits for them!

Having prepared the duck, put the carrot and onion quarters with the parsley sprig inside the cavity, and then be generous with a sprinkling of sea salt and freshly ground black pepper on the breast flesh. Put the bird, breast upwards, on a rack set in or over a small roasting tin (the main photo shows one duck uncooked and the other cooked). Put the bird into the

pre-heated oven and cook for 1 hour; turn the oven down to gas mark 7, 425°F (220°C) and cook for a further 30 minutes. Every 15 minutes, take the tin out of the oven and, handling it with extreme care, pour off any fat that may have collected on the base. To do this I hold the corner of the tin in my working hand and use my other gloved hand to hold the bird, quickly disposing of the fat in the warmed Pyrex bowl. A normal duck can produce over 5 fl oz (150 ml) of useful fat. If this is left to build up in the roasting tin, the contents would begin to steam slightly, and produce a soggy skin.

To portion the bird, use your gloved hands to transfer it to a carving board, and place breast-side up. With a large carving knife cut the duck in half, sawing through the centre bone (photo 1). This does require a degree of force. Lay both halves flat on the board and then cut diagonally through each so that you have two leg and two breast portions (photo 2). The rib cage can then easily be removed from underneath the breast and put to one side for eventual use in a stockpot.

Garnish each duck portion with an orange wedge speared through with a cocktail stick holding a cherry and a large sprig of parsley (photo 3). I don't usually serve a gravy with this dish, but a spoonful of the following stuffing certainly enhances it deliciously.

Duck stuffing

2 oz (50 g) butter
4 oz (100 g) onions, peeled and finely chopped
4 oz (100 g) duck and chicken livers, chopped
1 level tablespoon chopped parsley
2 oz (50 g) breadcrumbs
2 oz (50 g) Cheddar cheese, grated
finely grated rind and juice of 1 orange
8 orange segments, roughly chopped

Melt the butter in a frying-pan and fry the onions until golden. Add the chopped duck and chicken livers with the parsley, breadcrumbs, cheese, orange rind and juice, and cook until dry (photo 4). Then simply fold in the orange segments. You can prepare this in advance and transfer it to a small ovenproof container to re-heat in the oven during the last 20 minutes of the duck's cooking time.

1 To portion the cooked duck, saw through the centre bone with a carving knife.

2 Lay both halves on the board and cut diagonally through each to make four portions.

3 A garnish of an orange wedge, cherry and parsley sprig adds the final touch.

4 For a separate 'stuffing' to serve with the duck, cook the ingredients together until fairly dry.

AND TO DRINK

I particularly recommend a wine made from the Merlot grape, as it stands up well to the richness of this dish.

Steamed vegetables

Vegetables and Salads

*T*HERE ARE TWO SCHOOLS *of thought when it comes to the steaming of vegetables. Many home economists and food technologists come way out in favour of this method of cooking because of the minimal loss of vitamins and proteins. Others say the vegetables finish up extremely bland and are too 'wet'. I have mixed feelings on the subject, but, after spending a great deal of time experimenting, I have come to four basic conclusions:*

1. *Great care must be taken over the buying of the vegetables.*

2. *Even greater attention than usual must be given to their preparation.*

3. *Practically every cooked vegetable is the better for having a strongish flavouring added.*

4. *Timing is of the utmost importance.*

Each year I judge various heats of a Junior Cook of the Year competition. In all, 45 of the 100 marks are allocated to the final taste – and, lo and behold, many accomplished budding cooks fail at this stage. The same applies to the new methods of growing, storing, distributing and selling of fresh fruit and vegetables. It is the end product in the consumer's mouth that should be of absolutely prime importance, but somewhere along the line big producers often lose sight of this point, and few vegetables these days are as truly seasonal – or as truly flavoursome – as they were 20 to 30 years ago. So, become a much more discriminating shopper and sampler, and rebel with your purse on your next shopping trip if you find a product lacking in taste.

Use a proper steamer if you have one, or, as I describe on p. 56, improvise with a colander, a saucepan and a tight-fitting lid to cover the food. For steam-cooking, it is essential that each individual piece of vegetable is the same size (photos 1–4). The following list gives an idea of timings and flavouring for 4 oz (100 g) prepared portions of different vegetables. In all cases they should be cooked over a base half-filled with boiling, well-salted water. Remember to be generous with the individual flavourings.

1 Broccoli and cauliflower should be broken into equal-sized pieces.

2 Carrots and other root vegetables, such as turnips, should be cut into batons of 2–3 in (5–7.5 cm) long.

3 Using scissors is the easy way to top and tail Kenya French beans.

4 The tough stalks need to be removed from spinach leaves for a number of dishes.

BEANSPROUTS:
Swill around in cold water, drain well, then cook for 2 minutes. Flavour with soy sauce.

BROAD BEANS:
Pod and skin (see p. 111), flavour with finely grated lemon rind, then cook for 1 minute.

BROCCOLI:
Break the florets into the size shown in photo 1, flavour with toasted sesame seeds and cook for 3 minutes.

BRUSSELS SPROUTS:
Use medium sprouts, trim and season with black pepper. Cook for 4 minutes.

CARROTS:
Peel large ones, slice then cut into batons as in photo 2. Season with slivers of preserved ginger and cook for 4 minutes.

CAULIFLOWER:
Break into florets as in photo 1, sprinkle with grated Parmesan cheese and cook for 3 minutes.

CELERY:
Cut into 3 in (7.5 cm) sticks, dab with wholegrain mustard and cook for 3 minutes.

FENNEL:
Cut individual leaves into slices, spike with Pernod and cook for 4 minutes.

KENYA FRENCH BEANS:
Top and tail the easy way (photo 3), then season with black pepper and cook for 4 minutes.

MUSHROOM CAPS:
Wipe, then sprinkle with fresh marjoram and cook for 2 minutes.

NEW POTATOES:
Scrub even-sized small potatoes, sprinkle with fresh mint and cook for 10–12 minutes.

OLD POTATOES:
Cut to the size of a circle of thumb and forefinger, peel, then flavour and cook as above.

RUNNER BEANS:
String, cut into 2 in (5 cm) lengths, flavour with fresh basil and cook for 4 minutes.

SPINACH LEAVES:
Wash, remove the tough stalks (photo 4), then flavour with finely grated orange rind and cook for 2 minutes.

SWEETCORN (BABY):
Trim and cut into halves or thirds, depending on size. Dab with butter and cook for 4 minutes.

TURNIP:
Peel, cut into ¼ in (5 mm) batons (photo 2), sprinkle with fresh fennel sprigs and cook for 3 minutes.

Vegetable pasta

*O*CCASIONALLY PEOPLE SAY *to me, 'How can you call this a pasta dish when there is no pasta in it?' I suppose they have a point. Perhaps one day the Trades Description Officer will descend upon me – until then I'll continue to call it vegetable pasta.*

It makes a delicious light supper dish, or can be served, coated with Roquefort sauce (see below), as a starter to a simple dinner party. The basic vegetables can also be coated with mayonnaise or warmed through in an oven with a farm egg broken over them. They can be stuffed into lettuce leaves and rolled up to look like a large sausage – very good for a 'finger buffet'. Or, for somebody convalescing after an illness, they can simply be served with warmed nutmeg milk or consommé.

The vegetables not only look attractive if scattered over poached or baked fish, but also provide a contrasting texture. I have a friend who plonks them into ramekins, fills these with lime jelly and tops them off with curried mayonnaise and toasted desiccated coconut!

The actual cutting up of the vegetables (known as 'julienne' in grand kitchens) does take time and patience, so make yourself comfortable. It can be done sitting down at the kitchen table; brew yourself a large pot of tea or coffee – or, better still, indulge in a tumbler of your cooking wine – and off you go.

Peppers, carrots, courgettes, leeks, parsnips, celery, turnip, mangetouts and runner beans can all be used for this dish, but try to remember that each vegetable, when prepared, should be as near the same thickness and length as possible.

Wipe peppers clean with a damp cloth, cut in half lengthways, remove and discard the seeds and any surplus white inside flesh, and top and tail. Lay each pepper half flat on the work surface and, using a small, sharp-pointed knife, cut it into thin 'shoelace' strips (photo 1).

Carrots should be the thick type. After peeling, topping and tailing, cut them to the same length as the red pepper strips and square the sides (all the good left-over bits should be used for stock-making). Cut into thin slices and then strips (photo 2).

The same has to be done with all the other vegetables you are using – and remember that similar thickness and length is essential for each variety. There is quite a waste, but left-over pieces can be simmered in stock, liquidised and used as a cream of vegetable soup. (See the section on soups.)

The vegetable strips have then to be blanched and refreshed – in other words, dunked into boiling salted water for a minute and then immediately dowsed under the cold running tap to arrest their cooking. The easiest way to do this is to get a large saucepan which will take your chip basket with ease, fill it two-thirds full with water and bring to the boil. Add a couple of teaspoons of salt, put each vegetable in turn into the chip basket and dunk in the boiling water (photo 3). Turn the vegetables out on to a dry tea towel or kitchen paper. Leave the blanched vegetables in the following marinades for 24 hours.

PEPPERS: _____
French dressing (see p. 168).

CARROTS: _____
Preserved ginger and its syrup.

COURGETTES: _____
Finely grated orange rind and juice.

LEEKS: _____
Wholegrain mustard with a little wine.

PARSNIPS: _____
Natural yoghurt with grated nutmeg.

CELERY: _____
Natural yoghurt with tomato purée.

TURNIP: _____
Honey and lemon juice.

MANGETOUTS: _____
Mint dressing.

RUNNER BEANS: _____
Melted butter with lots of freshly ground black pepper.

When you wish to serve the vegetables, take them out of their marinades and mix together in a large bowl (photo 4).

To serve them with the Roquefort sauce mentioned above, divide into dishes in portions of 3–4 oz (75–100 g), and gently warm through. Put 2 table-spoons double cream per person into a small saucepan and bring quickly to the boil. Cook for a couple of minutes, then add 1 oz (25 g) grated Roquefort cheese per person. Stir until combined. Pour over the vegetable portions and add a sprinkling of chopped herbs or toasted sesame or sunflower seeds.

1 With a very sharp knife, cut the de-seeded pepper halves into very fine strips.

2 Thick carrots should be squared, then cut into slices and julienne strips.

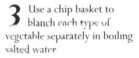

3 Use a chip basket to blanch each type of vegetable separately in boiling salted water

4 After separate marination, bring the vegetable pasta together, then divide between individual dishes.

AND TO DRINK

Frascati is ideal, or a glass of sparkling dry white wine.

Vegetable casserole

VEGETABLES ARE OFTEN the point where cooks come unstuck: greens that seem to have done a turn in the washing machine; root vegetables not al dente, just uncooked. One usually has many things to think about when folk come round for a meal, so this recipe and the one following will help you to serve unusual vegetables easily — they can be prepared even 24 hours ahead of time. Yes, I know the food purists will be screaming about lost vitamins — far rather these diminish than the hosts lose their cool!

Use root vegetables of your choice to suit your budget, but do try to include celeriac or salsify occasionally. When Jerusalem artichokes are available, I always like to use a few of those.

The casserole could be topped with cheese sauce instead of the breadcrumbs used here before being flashed under the grill. It could also be prepared in individual dishes. If you have any beansprouts in the larder, marinate these in your favourite French dressing for a few hours and then scatter them over the grilled topping. Or you could use hazelnuts — ring the changes! A large spoonful of thick yoghurt mixed with chopped herbs is delicious too, as is a large dollop of cream sauce (see p. 164).

Serves 6 generously

3 lb (1.3 kg) assorted root vegetables

4 oz (100 g) softened butter

1–2 oz (25–50 g) garlic cloves, peeled and crushed to a paste with 2 teaspoons salt

8 oz (225 g) onions, peeled and finely diced

freshly ground black pepper

1 pint (600 ml) strong chicken or vegetable stock (see p. 10)

4 oz (100 g) savoury breadcrumbs (see p. 49)

Pre-heat the oven to gas mark 4, 350°F (180°C).

It is important that, after peeling, the vegetables are prepared with care (photo 1). They should all be more or less the same small cube size (leeks will naturally be in thinnish circles).

Melt half the butter in a large frying-pan and cook the garlic and onions, then transfer to an ovenproof dish — I usually use an 8 in (20 cm) diameter oval Pyrex casserole with a lid. Fry the vegetable cubes in the same pan, making sure that the butter sizzles all

1 For the vegetable casserole, the vegetables should be prepared carefully and cut to the same small cube size.

2 Once you have sealed the vegetables in butter, and they are ready to cook in the oven, cover with stock.

3 Before serving, top the casserole with savoury breadcrumbs and brown under the grill.

the time – you need to *seal* them. If you put too many cubes in the pan at once, the heat will drastically reduce and instead of sealing you will be steaming them.

Before transferring each cooked batch of vegetables to the casserole, grind on fresh black pepper to taste, bearing in mind that root vegetables are invariably slightly sweet. Keep adding a little more of the butter to the pan as necessary to finish off frying them. When all are in the casserole, give them a good stir together. If you are preparing the dish way ahead of time, simply cover and leave somewhere cool.

Pour the stock over the vegetables in the casserole (photo 2), cover and cook for 45 minutes in the pre-heated oven.

Near the end of the cooking time, heat the grill. When the casserole is cooked, carefully remove it from the oven, top with the breadcrumbs and finish off under the hot grill (photo 3).

AND TO DRINK

With a main-course vegetable casserole, serve a glass of your favourite sherry, well chilled.

Root vegetable purées

*O*NCE AGAIN, *these can be made in advance of the meal. Any root vegetable is suitable, as well as Brussels sprouts.*

Serves 6

1 lb (450 g) vegetable of your choice, prepared and diced

salt

5 fl oz (150 ml) double cream

Cook the vegetable dice until soft in salted water, then drain and dry well. Place in a food processor, add the cream and blend to a purée. Always pass the purée through a sieve (I use a soup ladle to do this as it is easier) into the top part of a double saucepan or into a Christmas-pudding bowl. Heat through in the double saucepan or in a bain-marie in the oven at gas mark 4, 350°F (180°C), for 15–20 minutes.

In the main photograph, along with the large portion of vegetable casserole (in the top left corner), you can see a purée of carrots with chopped preserved ginger, a parsnip purée with toasted pine kernels, and a purée of Brussels sprouts with chopped hazelnuts.

Rösti potatoes

THE POTATO IS POSSIBLY the world's most popular vegetable – amazingly enough, it virtually equals the wheat crop in both volume and value! It was introduced into this country by Sir Walter Raleigh in 1584 and, despite the bad press it so often receives, it is surely here to stay.

Potatoes cannot be fattening as they are 80 per cent water! I admit the other 20 per cent is nearly all starch, but what gives them such an undeserved bad name is the oil in which they are often fried or the butter put on top of them. It could be argued that, when organically grown, they actually promote health because of their high potassium content.

Six to seven million tons of potatoes are grown and consumed in this country each year – all controlled by the Potato Marketing Board – which means that on average we each eat 230 lb (104 kg) annually! Many are used in processed foods, though. Crisps, for instance, were invented in the American town of Saratoga Springs way back in 1853 by a Red Indian chef. His family would be millionaires today if he had been able to patent his invention, as in this country alone over 100 million packets are sold every single week of the year. (They are not so decadent as you think: each bag contains less salt than a slice of white bread, and six times the vitamin C of an apple!)

Rösti is a marvellous supper dish and goes well with a thick rasher of bacon or a slice of liver. Once you have got the knack, you can vary the recipe virtually endlessly, adding cheese, cooked onions, or whatever you fancy. Rösti has to be prepared immediately before cooking and eating, otherwise it will not be firm and crisp.

1 Peel the potatoes thinly and grate quickly and coarsely into a bowl.

2 Press the grated potatoes firmly down in the pan with a fish slice to form into a cake. Don't let it stick, though.

3 For fanned roast potatoes, slice through – but not fully – for this cock's comb effect.

4 Pin the potatoes into the fanned position with wooden cocktail sticks.

Serves 4

1 lb (450 g) large King Edward potatoes

3 oz (75 g) softened butter

salt and freshly ground black pepper

Peel the potatoes very thinly (most of the goodness is near the skin) and grate them quickly and coarsely (photo 1). Melt half the butter in a thick-bottomed or non-stick frying pan with a base of at least 8 in (20 cm) diameter.

Lightly season the grated potatoes, turn the heat up and throw them into the pan. With a fish slice or palette knife, keep pressing the potatoes down and bringing them in from the edge of the pan. You need to make all the bits stick together to form a cake, so be firm, making them sizzle (photo 2). At the same time you should keep easing the slice underneath to ensure that nothing is sticking to the base of the pan.

Cook for 4 minutes and then dot the remaining butter on top. Turn the cake over. Press down and cook for a further 4 minutes and the dish is done. Turn out on to a board and portion using a serrated knife. Serve at once.

Fanned roast potatoes

*N*O SELF-RESPECTING *joint can hold its head high unless these fanned roast potatoes are served alongside it – particularly if you have good beef dripping or duck or goose fat to cook them in! King Edwards are again best for this, but use smaller ones than for rösti. All the fat goes up through the slits for the finest roast spuds you ever tasted.*

Pre-heat the oven to gas mark 6, 400°F (200°C), and heat your chosen fat in an ovenproof dish.

Peel the potatoes very thinly, and slice through three-quarters of the way to form a cock's comb effect (photo 3). Spread the 'slices' out as far as they will go (like a hand of playing cards) and fix in the fanned position with wooden cocktail sticks (photo 4).

Put the fanned potatoes into boiling salted water and bring back to the boil. Cook for 2 minutes only. Drain and dry, then put into the hot fat and into the oven for 40 minutes, turning them after the first 15. Remember to remove the cocktail sticks before serving.

Jerusalem artichokes

*T*HEY SHARE THE SAME NAME, but the globe and the Jerusalem artichoke are quite unrelated. Both look exotic, but they're easy to grow and delicious to eat (the globe also looks wonderful in a herbaceous border).

The Jerusalem artichoke, a root tuber native to North America and greatly prized by the Red Indians, was introduced to Europe in the early seventeenth century. It was called 'artichoke' not because it is related to the globe type, but because its flavour was thought to be like that of the globe's heart (they are not at all similar in my opinion). The 'Jerusalem' part of its name is a corruption of the Italian girasole, meaning sunflower, or 'turning to the sun'; the Jerusalem artichoke is related to the sunflower.

The skin should be white or purplish; avoid any that are green or too dirty. Scrub the artichokes well and, if they're smooth, you can peel them thinly if you wish. If you opt for peeling, drop them immediately into acidulated water to prevent discoloration. However, I think the best flavour is near the skin, so recommend cooking them with the skins on. They may not look too attractive, but they taste delicious.

To cook Jerusalem artichokes, boil or steam them. Keep the water in which they've boiled as this will be full of flavour and can be used as the basis for a soup or sauce (it sometimes sets to a jelly when cold).

Jerusalem artichokes have a very distinct, unusual flavour. They make a wonderful soup — Palestine Soup is a classic, re-emphasising the mistaken Jerusalem connection; lovely smooth cream purées go well with beef or poultry; chips or fritters are crunchy on the outside, soft within; a soufflé is a delicate delight. Jerusalem artichokes can be roasted like potatoes or eaten raw when young and tender — the flesh is sweet and nutty. Cook with other vegetables that aren't too strong in flavour — leeks rather than onions, for instance.

Jerusalem artichokes with fried bacon, onion and garlic

Serves 4

1 tablespoon oil

4 oz (100 g) bacon, de-rinded and diced

4 oz (100 g) onions, peeled and finely chopped

2 garlic cloves, peeled and crushed

12 oz (350 g) Jerusalem artichokes, scrubbed and diced

Bring the oil to smoking point in a frying-pan and add the bacon, onions and garlic. Cook for 4 minutes or until slightly golden.

Add the artichokes and stir-fry for between 8 and 12 minutes, depending on whether you like them crisp, soft or 'in between'.

Globe artichokes

GLOBE ARTICHOKES HAVE BEEN *cultivated in Europe for thousands of years. The Romans and Greeks enjoyed them, and Elizabethan England was reintroduced to them by Italian imports. Catherine de Medici, who took them with her from Italy to France, was considered rather 'fast' by the French court when she ate them (to bursting point, apparently) as they were thought to be an aphrodisiac.*

The globe artichoke is one of the most elegant and delicious of vegetables, and makes an ideal starter, either hot or cold. The part eaten is the young, immature flower head: the base of the leaves is scraped off with the teeth, and the fond *(bottom or heart) is separated from the leaves and the 'choke', and eaten with a knife and fork. The hairy fronds of the inedible central choke would eventually become the purple thistle-like flower.*

In Britain, despite being popular until the end of the nineteenth century, the globe artichoke seemed to disappear until the 1960s. A Scottish friend, coming to London in 1967, had to be shown how to eat them at a posh dinner party, much to her embarrassment. Perhaps that's why they fell from favour – they *are a lot of work.*

Before cooking, plunge the artichoke head-down into salted water to get rid of any dirt or insect life. Remove the stem and any untidy or damaged bottom leaves.

Cook in lots of boiling salted water – with vinegar or lemon juice added if you like – for 30–50 minutes, depending on size. (Never cook in an iron or aluminium pot as these can discolour.) Test when the cooking time is nearly up: if a leaf comes away easily, the artichoke is cooked.

I like artichokes best as a starter, when I can take off the leaves one by one, dip them hot into melted (plain or lemon) butter or hollandaise sauce, or cold into vinaigrette, with the anticipation of the delicious *fond* to come.

Cooked artichokes can also be stuffed, after the hairy choke has been scraped away, with a variety of fillings – mushroom pâté (see p. 27) would be good. The hearts themselves can be used in many other ways – in salads, with *antipasto*, fried in butter, in quiches and in purées.

If you are cooking the artichokes only for the hearts, scrape off the leaf flesh to add to a delicately flavoured dressing or mayonnaise – waste not, want not.

From *A Feast of Vegetables* by John Tovey (Century).

AND TO DRINK

With the Jerusalem artichoke dish, I would drink a well chilled rosé.

Potato and mushroom flan

———◦❖◦———

T OWARDS THE END of each autumn I endeavour to spend some time in Provence with friends who have a delightful vineyard and old farmhouse which they have turned into a base for their photography business. A few of us descend and have what we call a good old flop! Breakfast is a self-service occasion in the sunny kitchen, we take it in turns to shop in the local village markets and to supply simple fare for longish, indulged luncheons sleeping it all off round the pool each afternoon. Evenings are spent at several Michelin restaurants but the one I like best is a very small, shabby establishment in the local village serving the simplest suppers. I nigh swooned when he produced a fresh truffle and cèpe tart – this is a very downmarket, but effective reproduction of the dish!

1 Slice the peeled potatoes as thinly as possible, then fry on *one side* only.

2 Line the base and sides of a flan tin with overlapping partly cooked potato slices, cooked side down.

3 When the flan is cooked, push up the loose bottom of the tin and slide the flan on to a serving plate.

Serves 6

1 lb (450 g) large potatoes, peeled

5 tablespoons olive oil

3 oz (75 g) butter

8 oz (225 g) onions, peeled and finely diced

1 oz (25 g) fresh garlic, peeled and crushed to a paste with 1 teaspoon salt

1 teaspoon ground cumin (optional)

10 oz (275 g) mushrooms, wiped and finely chopped or sliced

5 fl oz (150 ml) double cream

1 egg plus 1 egg yolk

Lay a sheet of tinfoil on the oven shelf you are going to use and pre-heat the oven to gas mark 6, 400°F (200°C). Have ready an 8 in (20 cm) loose-bottomed flan tin.

Slice the potatoes as thinly as possible (photo 1). Gently heat 2 tablespoons of the olive oil in a frying-pan, add 1 oz (25 g) of the butter and, when combined, fry 10 oz (275 g) of the potatoes until golden-brown *on one side only* – transferring them as you cook to a tray spread with a double thickness of kitchen paper to drain off the fat. Keep the remaining uncooked potatoes to one side.

Starting in the middle of the flan tin, arrange the part-cooked potato slices, cooked side down, on the base, overlapping in larger and larger circles (photo 2) and building them up round the sides until they just come above the top. You must overlap the slices completely, otherwise the egg custard will leak out.

Use about 7 oz (200 g) of the part-cooked potatoes for the base and sides of the tin and reserve the rest.

Put the remaining olive oil into the same frying-pan and, when hot, add the remaining butter in little knobs. Cook the finely chopped onions with the crushed garlic until golden. Add the ground cumin (if using), then the mushrooms, and cook for a few more minutes. Drain on another tray lined with kitchen paper and divide this mixture into three.

Scatter one-third of the mushroom mixture over the potato base and cover this with half the remaining thinly sliced *uncooked* potatoes. Repeat with another layer of mushrooms, then one of uncooked potatoes, ending with the last of the mushroom mixture.

Beat the cream with the egg and egg yolk and pour over the final layer of mushrooms. You will still have 3 oz (75 g) part-cooked potatoes which you should now layer on top of the flan, cooked side up, to form a pie crust (main picture).

Put the prepared flan on the foil-covered oven shelf and cook for 45 minutes. Remove from oven and leave to settle for 5 minutes. Take out of the flan case (photo 3) and cut into six generous wedges.

AND TO DRINK

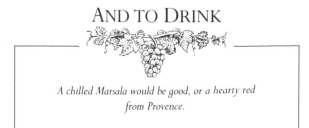

A chilled Marsala would be good, or a hearty red from Provence.

Ratatouille

*T*HERE MUST BE NEARLY *as many recipes for this Provençal dish as there are for shortbread. Some insist on using green instead of red peppers; some say garlic is optional, whereas others claim it is essential; sometimes everything is piled into a casserole and simply cooked slowly in the oven. I have read that the dish should be cooked only in the autumn when the ingredients are cheaper, or in early summer when the vegetables are young and bursting with flavour. One cookery writer puts sliced potatoes in hers (heaven forbid!), and another suggests baby mushrooms which would be completely lost in this robust dish. All, however, are in complete and absolute agreement that olive oil must be used – once again, one that suits your purse and palate.*

I must admit that when I first do this dish each year, I quiver with joy, and it is served immediately accompanied by

some cold Lakeland lamb, a leg which has been liberally studded with garlic before being roasted. Years ago, when I first discovered ratatouille and I was asked what was for lunch, I stuttered in my excitement and the word came out as 'rat-er-ter-tui'; this it has been called ever since! The aroma of the dish, the beautiful combination of the different textures and colours of the vegetables – it's all wonderful. Normally I am one for plating each and every course I serve to guests, but this is the only exception, particularly as I have discovered the splendid non-stick, two-handled frying pan shown in the main picture. It is simply taken straight off the hob and put on an iron trivet on the table over a couple of stout table mats, and the dish is up for grabs. I tell you now, it will stop even the most stimulating conversation, and all you will hear are sensuous groans of pleasure and appreciation!

Serve the ratatouille by itself. If you should ever have any left over, portion it into individual ramekins and then bake an egg on top of each.

Serves 4 generously

8 oz (225 g) firm aubergines

free-running salt

6 tablespoons good-quality olive oil

1 oz (25 g) soft butter

4 fresh garlic cloves, crushed to a paste with 2 teaspoons salt

8 oz (225 g) onions, peeled and finely chopped

4 oz (100 g) fennel, finely chopped

12 oz (350 g) red peppers

6 oz (175 g) green peppers

8 oz (225 g) small courgettes

1 1/2 lb (700 g) firm tomatoes

2–3 tablespoons finely chopped fresh herbs (parsley, basil, tarragon, oregano, as available)

freshly ground black pepper

Wipe the aubergines with a damp cloth, trim the ends and slice into 1/4 in (5 mm) circles. Cut these into strips, then lay them on a cooling rack over a double thickness of kitchen paper. Sprinkle generously with salt (photo 1) and leave for at least 1 1/2 hours for the sour liquid to drain away. At the end of this time, pat the strips dry with kitchen paper.

In a large frying pan heat 4 tablespoons of the olive oil with the butter and in this gently cook the crushed garlic, chopped onions and fennel until golden. Do not let them burn.

Cut the red and green peppers in half lengthways, discard the seeds and stalk, then slice very thinly (photo 2). Wipe the courgettes, top and tail them and, using a scorer, make channelled indentations lengthways (photo 3). Slice them thinly. Skin the tomatoes and remove the seeds (see p. 169), then coarsely chop the flesh.

When the onions and fennel are cooked to your liking, add the thinly sliced peppers and slowly simmer for 10 minutes. Add the balance of the oil and the dried aubergine strips and cook for a further 10 minutes. Next add the sliced courgettes and give the dish a further 5 minutes of simmering. Add the tomatoes (photo 4) and, once you have warmed these through, it is time to go mad with your freshly

1 Sprinkle the aubergine strips with salt and leave to drain of sour liquid.

2 Halve, de-seed, then slice the peppers very thinly.

3 Using a scorer, make indentations lengthways in the courgettes before slicing – the slices will then be much more decorative.

4 Add the skinned, de-seeded and chopped tomatoes to the ratatouille.

chopped herbs and ground pepper until you get a flavour to your particular taste. Always *taste*, add, then taste again – one of the cook's perks! (I must admit that I often use as many as 4 tablespoons fresh mixed garden herbs as I really want the dish to reek of them, without their 'taking over'.) Serve immediately.

AND TO DRINK

I find a young Beaujolais, which has been slightly chilled, the ideal wine to go with this dish.

Meat-stuffed cabbage

*W*HEN I WAS A KID *a dozen of these were made mid-week — when the ready cash was dwindling fast, and pay-night wasn't until Friday — and then were sold by the lady who ran the corner shop in Norfolk Street in Barrow-in-Furness. Most were bought by 'regulars' in and around the area, and each Monday lunchtime it was my job to go knocking on doors asking for the muslin back! For they were cooked in muslin, suspended at various levels from sticks which criss-crossed a boiling cauldron of seasoned water. It was also my task laboriously to hand-mince the left-over meats to make them and, using the then new-fangled, small, but extremely sharp metal roller, cut up the parsley and whatever other herbs were available.*

The following recipe is much easier to cope with in a modern kitchen, and once you have taken to it the variations are endless. Chicken, lamb, beef and game may be used as the meat base, and as far as the vegetarian version goes, the sky is virtually the limit. If you decide to vary the meat version, though, I would respectfully suggest that before you put the stuffing into the cabbage leaves, you take a small spoonful out of the mix and quickly fry it off in a touch of butter. When it's cooked, taste it and, if you feel it could do with a little lift, add some mustard, chutney, horseradish, Worcestershire sauce, curry essence or perhaps more herbs.

The dish is delicious served with lots of runny apple or tomato sauce.

Serves 6

3–4 outer green cabbage leaves

softened butter for greasing

8 oz (225 g) belly pork

8 oz (225 g) lean pork (preferably from the leg)

2 garlic cloves, peeled and crushed to a paste with a little salt

12 green peppercorns (the sort marinated in brine)

1 dessertspoon white wine vinegar

2 teaspoons chopped fresh herbs (preferably rosemary, sage, oregano and mint, or whatever is available)

about 10 good grindings of black pepper

1 large egg, lightly beaten

Pre-heat the oven to gas mark 3, 325°F (160°C), and rub the inside of a pudding bowl (2 pints/1.2 litres, or less) with butter.

Remove the stalks from the cabbage leaves and blanch the leaves in boiling salted water for 4 minutes. Then plunge them immediately into a bowl of cold water to set the colour. Drain and pat dry with a clean cloth or kitchen paper. Line the buttered bowl with the leaves, making sure that they overlap well (photo 1) to form a good outer shell for your dish. You also want to make sure you have sufficient left at the top to fold over when the mixture is inserted.

Finely mince the belly and lean pork (don't use a food processor), and put this in a bowl with all the other ingredients, using the lightly beaten egg to hold the mix together. It is important that all the ingredients are evenly distributed.

Put this stuffing into the cabbage-lined bowl, gently press down, and then bring the leaf ends over to hide the meat mix (photo 2). Cover with a large square of muslin (or a piece of clean old sheet or pillowcase) and securely tie this on. Put a small saucer or plate on top and on top of this a 2 lb (900 g) weight (photo 3). Place the bowl in a deep roasting tin, surround with boiling water to come half-way up the sides of the tin and cook in the pre-heated oven for 2 hours.

Remove the weight and muslin, and turn out on to a plate (photo 4). Cut into wedges and serve hot.

1 Line a buttered bowl carefully with the blanched cabbage leaves, overlapping them well.

2 Press the meat mixture into the cabbage-lined bowl and bring up the overhanging ends of the leaves to enclose the stuffing.

3 Tie a cloth on to the bowl and place a saucer or plate and a weight on top before cooking.

4 Remove weight, plate and cloth, then turn out to serve.

Vegetarian stuffed cabbage

Serves 6

softened butter

3–4 outer green cabbage leaves, trimmed and blanched as in the preceding recipe

4 oz (100 g) fresh spinach leaves, trimmed and blanched as cabbage, but for 2 minutes only

4 oz (100 g) lettuce leaves, coarsely chopped

2 oz (50 g) onions, peeled and finely chopped

2 garlic cloves, peeled and crushed to a paste with a little salt

4 oz (100 g) shelled walnuts, coarsely chopped

2 oz (50 g) ground hazelnuts

2 oz (50 g) strong Cheddar cheese, finely grated

salt and freshly ground black pepper

2 tablespoons finely chopped herbs

1 egg, beaten with 3 tablespoons double cream

4 sage leaves

Line a pudding bowl with the cabbage leaves exactly as described in the preceding recipe and then line again with the blanched spinach leaves, making a thicker outer layer.

Thoroughly combine all the other ingredients except the sage. Fill the lined pudding bowl with the mix, place the sage leaves on top and then bring up the edges of the cabbage leaves and cover with muslin as in the preceding recipe. Cook in the same way – at the same temperature, but for 1¼ hours only – and serve similarly.

AND TO DRINK

A chilled Beaujolais would go well with both dishes.

Seasonal salads

*S*ALADS SHOULD BE *as much fun to make and eat as are the French dressings to accompany them (see p. 168). And do remember that the latter can be served cold or warm.*

Get out of the habit of serving your salads on a flat dinner plate and go for individual bowl portions, which will mean that every guest gets a little of each item. Some of the imported wooden salad bowls are not only relatively inexpensive, but also very good for this type of dish, though cereal or soup bowls from your dinner service will suffice. Paint the bowls lightly with a good-quality oil and then press and pulp half a peeled garlic clove on the base and up the sides. This is a very easy task if you use the wooden bowls as a heavy pestle will soon do the job; a soup spoon should be used on china.

Lettuces come in endless sorts, shapes and sizes, and some of the multiple stores sell very interesting assorted mini-packs. John Gerard, the famous sixteenth-century herbalist, wrote about lettuce that 'It cooleth the heat of the stomach called heartburn, quencheth thirst and causeth sleep.' It does none of these for me, but it is a well-known fact that the milky juice of the lettuce contains a small trace of an alkaloid similar to that found in the opium poppy – so beware!

Spinach, watercress, mustard and cress and cabbage leaves are also very good bases for salads (rocket, though rare, is a joy too), and the addition of a good teaspoon of chopped mixed fresh herbs per person is a revelation.

If you can get hold of rape from a local farm, you will find that the flowers are not only colourful but also edible and sweet. Borage flowers add a delightful splash of colour too, as do nasturtium flowers and chrysanthemum petals, I am told!

Skinned tomatoes (see p. 169) can be added in quarters, but I prefer to remove the seeds and then chop the flesh coarsely. Red and yellow peppers (I find the green indigestible) should be cut into thin rings and these cut into very small pieces.

Cucumber should be wiped and split lengthways. Take out the seeds and then once again chop finely. Hard-boiled eggs should be coarsely grated or passed through a sieve.

Peeled and grated raw carrots are enhanced with a little finely chopped preserved ginger and its juice, together with a small dollop of natural yoghurt. Mushrooms should be peeled, then have a warm French dressing poured over and left to get cold. Baked smoked bacon bits are delicious in many salads.

Many ingredients are the better for partly pre-cooking and then leaving to marinate. Very small cauliflower and broccoli florets, for example, should be cooked for a few minutes, then drained. Scatter the cauliflower, as it cools, with grated Parmesan cheese and toasted sesame seeds; sprinkle broccoli florets with raspberry vinegar.

The *pièce de résistance*, though, of any summer salad is the broad bean. It is a seemingly wasteful vegetable, I know, as one needs to buy at least 1 lb (450 g) to get only a handful. Remove the beans from the pods and cook slowly in salted water until they are just tender. Drain and refresh under a cold tap. Hold each bean in the thumb and first finger of your working hand, nip off the stalk end with your other thumb and first finger, and then with a little pressure pop out the dark green inside bean. The skinned beans, marinated in warmed bacon fat, are a feast in themselves.

Nuts are a useful salad ingredient, but should be toasted. Spread the shelled nuts on a baking tray and cook in the oven at gas mark 3, 325°F (160°C), until nice and golden. Put into your salad whole or coarsely chopped.

The very thin French beans are good when cooked in salted water and then drained and tossed in a generous portion of hot melted butter, with an equally generous grinding of black pepper. Mangetouts are delicious if topped and tailed, cut into very thin strips and covered with a fresh mint dressing; chill these in the fridge before serving.

Small cooked new potatoes should, while still hot, be liberally strewn with finely chopped chives and spring onions. Pour boiling French dressing over them and leave to cool.

I prefer fresh garden peas to be added to a salad simply raw. Cooked sweetcorn taken off the cob and then marinated in a mixture of honey and fresh lemon juice is tantalising.

Fruits are for more dishes than just 'fresh fruit salad and cream' – many are quite at home in seasonal salads. Thin Granny Smith apple wedges marinated in the juice and finely grated rind of a fresh lime are wonderful. Orange or grapefruit segments (see p. 15) are juicy and appealing. Diced avocado coated with toasted desiccated coconut adds a touch of the exotic.

Small croûtons normally associated with soup add a teasing texture to any salad. And the dish can be finished off with a radish 'flower' (photos 1–4 show how to make one).

1 To make a radish 'flower', start by cutting a tiny slice off the base of the radish so that it will stand firmly.

2 Cut four little trenches or lips across the top of the radish to create a decorative centre for the 'flowers'.

3 Make tiny carving cuts or slices round the radish to form 'petals'.

4 After chilling in iced water, these petals open up to form the radish 'flowers'.

AND TO DRINK

Salads always call for a cold Sauvignon Blanc.

Fresh oranges with caramel sauce

There are basically two types of oranges — the bitter or Seville (used for marmalades), and the sweet or China orange. Nowadays, there is never a month when these fruit are not available in the UK as they are grown in abundance in Florida, Israel (Jaffas) and South Africa (Outspans), and in Spain and Italy, both of which produce the quite delicious seedless 'blood' orange.

In puddings oranges show off their numerous facets, whether as rind, juice or whole fruit. A small bowl of juicy orange segments with a few toasted almond flakes scattered on the top will finish off a simple meal for me; a few sprigs of freshly picked mint will enhance it, as will a drop of any orange-flavoured liqueur.

Serves 4

4 oranges, washed

Sauce

8 oz (225 g) soft light brown sugar

8 tablespoons single cream

2 oz (50 g) softened butter

Optional garnish

lightly sweetened double cream

flaked almonds, toasted

sprigs of mint

Remove the peel and pith from the oranges as if preparing segments (see p. 15). Reserve the peel.

Turn the prepared oranges on their sides and, using a serrated knife, slice them through to make about six to eight circles resembling bicycle wheels. Reassemble the oranges, holding the circles in place with wooden cocktail sticks (photo 1).

Put the sugar, cream and butter in a thick-based saucepan and cook over a medium heat for at least 6 minutes, stirring all the time with a long-handled wooden spoon. After about 5 minutes the mixture should start to thicken.

Remove the sauce from the heat and stir vigorously for a while. As it sets and cools, pour it slowly over the oranges and leave to go cold. Garnish each orange, if you like, with lightly sweetened double cream, toasted almond flakes and sprigs of mint. Remember to remove the cocktail sticks before biting into the oranges.

1 Peel and slice the oranges, then reassemble the slices, using wooden cocktail sticks.

2 Cut the orange peel into ¼ in (5 mm) wide strips.

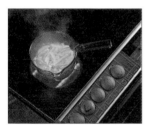

3 After bringing to the boil and refreshing in cold water at least four times, simmer the rind strips in stock syrup.

4 Dip one end of each candied orange peel strip into melted chocolate.

Make the stock syrup by bringing the sugar and water to the boil in a clean saucepan. Turn down to a simmer and add the softened orange peel strips (photo 3). Continue simmering until all the syrup has been absorbed.

Spread the strips on a cooling rack, and when they are completely cold, put them in a storage container kept in a cool place.

Put the chocolate and brandy or rum into a small heatproof bowl and suspend this over a saucepan of simmering water to melt the chocolate and combine it with the spirit. Dip one end of each candied orange peel strip into the chocolate (photo 4) and leave on a tray to set. These are delicious served either with the oranges in caramel sauce or with after-dinner coffee.

Candied orange strips

reserved orange peel

Stock syrup

6 oz (175 g) granulated sugar

3 fl oz (85 ml) water

Chocolate

4 oz (100 g) good-quality plain chocolate

1 tablespoon brandy or rum

To make an orange peel garnish, cut the reserved peel into ¼ in (5 mm) wide strips (photo 2). Put the strips in a saucepan, cover with water and bring to the boil. Tip the strips into a sieve and refresh with cold water. Repeat this process at least four times to soften rind.

Boozy oranges

Serves 4

4 oranges, washed

Syrup

8 oz (225 g) caster sugar

4 cloves

1 in (2.5 cm) cinnamon stick

2½ fl oz (65 ml) cold water

2 tablespoons each cooking brandy and liqueur of your taste

Prepare the oranges as in the first recipe, pinned together with cocktail sticks. Heat the syrup ingredients together in a pan and, when the sugar has melted, add the oranges. Poach them for 5 minutes, and then let them cool in the syrup. Remove the cocktail sticks from the oranges before serving.

AND TO DRINK

A chilled glass of Beaumes de Venise.

Summer pudding

*T*HIS HAS TO BE *the easiest pudding to make, and one that invariably has guests swooning over its taste and texture – particularly if, like me, you are still able to find a local supplier of the most splendid Jersey cream (mind you, I could settle for an enormous bowl of clotted Cornish!).*

The mistakes most people make when preparing this sweet are cutting the bread far too thick; stewing the fruit for too long and to a mush at the beginning; and serving it the next day. Seek out a good white loaf from a local baker and cut it thinly; barely cook the fruit; and leave the pudding(s) in the fridge for **at least** *2 whole days before serving!*

A few years ago, in August, I took half a dozen summer puds out to friends in Africa as hand luggage (what a performance getting them through Customs!). As the weather there was so appalling, I served home-made hot custard with them; my friends thought the dish fantastic, I thought it had been ruined!

The 'yardstick' I use for one pudding is basically 2 lb (900 g) summer fruits to 6 oz (175 g) caster sugar. While the definitive recipe given below is the one cooked at Miller Howe throughout the high summer season – normally served with a complimentary glass of home-made elderflower wine (see p. 121) – if you haven't got all these fruits, do not worry. Simply use more of another, always making sure that you end up with the 2 lb (900 g).

Some folk seem to think that a summer pudding can be made with fruit that is 'over the hill': nothing could be further from the truth. If you use cheap, soggy fruit, you will end up with a mixture more like jam than anything else. The fruit has to be fresh and firm, and I never wash it! Simply hull the strawberries and raspberries, and take the redcurrants and blackcurrants off their stalks. Both are simple tasks that call for a chair and possibly a glass of something . . . take your time and use your nimble fingers for hulling; a (preferably silver) fork will soon have the currants sliding off their firm stalks. The gooseberries I top and tail (using tapestry scissors) and the apples are peeled, cored and then sliced very thinly indeed.

Serves 8

8 oz (225 g) strawberries, hulled

8 oz (225 g) raspberries, hulled

4 oz (100 g) each redcurrants and blackcurrants, off the stalk

4 oz (100 g) sweet dessert gooseberries, topped and tailed

4 oz (100 g) dessert apples, peeled, cored and very thinly sliced

6 oz (175 g) caster sugar

softened butter

about 8 × ¼ in (5 mm) slices good white bread, crusts removed

Put the prepared fruit into a thick-bottomed saucepan and add the sugar. Over a low heat allow the fruit just to sweat and simply dissolve the sugar (photo 1). *Do not* bring to the boil and, whatever you do, do not overcook.

Rub the inside of a 1½ pint (900 ml) pudding bowl with butter. Shape one slice of bread to cover the base of the bowl and come just slightly up the sides (photo 2). Carefully overlap most of the other slices to cover the inside of the bowl completely, making sure that you leave no gaps (photo 3).

Gently pour the cooked fruit into the bread 'container', then use the remaining bread slices to make a lid (photo 4). Place on top an old saucer which will cover this bread topping, and on top of this put an 8 oz (225 g) weight. When cold, put in the fridge and leave to set for (preferably) 48 hours.

To turn the pudding out easily, slide a palette knife gently down between the side of the bowl and the bread (you will hear a slurping noise as the air works its way in). Invert the bowl carefully on a flat serving plate, and the pudding should slip out without damage. You can do this ahead of serving and simply put it back in the fridge covered with cling film until you need it, but once you cut the first portion, it will partially collapse.

1 Never overcook the soft fruit. Just allow to sweat, enough to dissolve the sugar and start the juices running.

2 Shape one slice of bread to cover the base of the buttered bowl.

3 Overlap most of the remaining slices so that the inside of the bowl is completely covered.

4 After the fruit has been poured into the bread 'container', cover with the remaining slices of bread as a lid.

AND TO DRINK

The drink I adore with summer pudding, when I am being terribly self-indulgent, is the light Italian liqueur, Frangelico, made from wild herbs and hazelnuts. It should be served frappé *(with lots of finely crushed ice).*

Hot fruit salad

*I*N THE EARLY SEVENTIES the restaurant in London was Lacy's, where Margaret Costa (food writer for the Sunday Times colour supplement and the American magazine Gourmet) reigned front of house, and her brilliant husband Bill Lacy ruled the kitchen brigade. The vaulted cellar, tiled floor and stark walls — relieved by some magnificent paintings — made for a somewhat noisy establishment, but one that was always heaving with folk hell-bent on enjoying themselves.

Margaret's obvious desire that every guest should thoroughly enjoy themselves was very apparent; but her mind was not geared to the horrible facts of plain, dull business, and she took it very personally when a customer complained. She would draw up a chair at the complainant's table, offer them a bottle of wine, and spend ages trying to talk them round. This often created havoc around her (to which she was totally oblivious), resulting in even more disgruntled diners! Her excellent but thought-provoking wine list was the talking point of the wine experts, as Margaret insisted that if somebody wanted to 'try a full bottle' they should be charged only for what they drank. Unfortunately, although the intention was brilliant, in practice it didn't work out: what wasn't allowed for was the amount the waiters could consume en route from table to cashier for charging, and so many guests were enraged to find their wine bill extremely high! Margaret would have been a sensational hit in a TV cookery series if only somebody had discovered her in her heyday at Lacy's and recorded those endless hilarious stories she told about the business.

Every time I prepare the following dish, Margaret comes to mind. One evening when I was at Lacy's, there was a really difficult French food snob at the next table who had led the staff a right dance all night. When confronted with the sweet menu, he asked in a loud voice, 'Wot ees an 'ot fruit salard?', not knowing that Margaret was right behind him. She towered over him in an immaculate silk creation and bouffant hairstyle, and riposted in an equally loud voice, 'Monsieur, an 'ot fruit salard is **a hot fruit salad,**' and swept away. He was served it, ate it and never said another word.

So often one can be tempted by what purports on menus to be 'fresh fruit salad'; the desire soon diminishes when one is confronted by mounds of thickly sliced, unpeeled Golden Delicious apples, what appear to be tinned orange and grapefruit segments, a few slices of kiwi fruit and tinned cherries. When making a fruit salad of your own, buy a little of everything that is available at your greengrocer's. A passion fruit will enhance it amazingly (photo 1 shows how the lovely juicy seeds are taken out). Grapes should be cut in half lengthways and the pips removed (photo 2). Peeled apples look prettier if 'balled' (photo 3) rather than plainly sliced. Bananas should be peeled and thinly sliced. Summer fruits should simply be hulled or removed from their stalks. Peaches, plums and nectarines can be cut into very thin wedges. Orange segments are a necessity (see p. 15 for how to segment citrus fruits), but don't use grapefruit as it is very sharp. Mango and papaya can be used in very small portions.

Make your fruit salad in a mixing bowl. Sprinkle some dark rum over it, then cover and leave for a few hours in the fridge.

Strain the mixed fruit, portion into small, straight-sided, heatproof ramekins and spread evenly with whipped cream. Cover this in turn with soft brown sugar (photo 4), put back in the fridge and chill again.

Pre-heat the grill to really hot and place the ramekins, on a baking tray, under the grill (as you would for a crème brûlée). Watch carefully while the sugar caramelises. Then transfer the baking tray to a hot hob to warm the bases of the dishes: this will take only about 2–3 minutes. Serve immediately. What could be simpler?

1 Cut the passion fruit in half and scrape out all the seeds and runny flesh with a spoon.

2 Cut grapes in half lengthways and remove the pips.

3 Balls of apple look much prettier than slices.

4 Cover the cream and fruit with soft brown sugar before grilling.

Apple sorbet

*S*ORBETS ARE REFRESHING *and satisfying and certainly not fattening and filling – which I must admit makes a change as far as my recipes go! However, I do find that the double cream used at the final stage of this recipe gives a much smoother and better-bodied end product. Any stick-in-the-mud traditionalists should use three egg whites, instead of just one, if they plan to leave the cream out. But how can they form an honest opinion if they don't try my method once? I felt immediately suspicious when I found a restaurateur in Paris using cream, but as soon as I ate the product I was totally convinced and converted. No diner has ever passed an adverse comment.*

The recipe is for an apple sorbet, but you can make many variations on this, utilising the same method and the same basic stock syrup below: use 3 lb (1.3 kg) puréed raw mango or melon flesh; 2½ lb (1.1 kg) soft summer fruit liquidised with 2 oz (50 g) icing sugar, then sieved to remove pips; or 2½ lb (1.1 kg) pears, prepared in the same way as the apples. To give further 'oomph' to the sorbets, add 6 tablespoons of the appropriate spirit to the purées: Calvados to the apple; rum to the mango; gin to the melon; Kirsch or brandy to the summer fruit; and Poire Williams to the pear.

You can also make a savoury sorbet – tomato and Pernod, which I serve after the main course and before the pudding. It is made in exactly the same way as the apple sorbet but using 3 lb (1.3 kg) soft tomatoes, liquidised, sieved and flavoured with 6 tablespoons Pernod.

Serves 10–12

2¹/₂ lb (1.1 kg) Granny Smith (or other) eating apples

4 tablespoons white wine or water

1 egg white plus 5 fl oz (150 ml) double cream, or 3 egg whites

Stock syrup

1 pint (600 ml) water

8 oz (225 g) cube sugar

rind and juice of 3 lemons

1 Wipe, slice and core the apples.

2 Simmer the apple in wine or water until soft, then purée.

3 Make a syrup with sugar, water, lemon rind and juice.

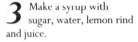

4 If using double cream, dribble in while the machine is running.

Wipe the apples, cut each into eight and discard the core sections (photo 1). Put in a saucepan with the wine or water and simmer until soft and sloppy (photo 2). Liquidise, pass through a sieve and allow to cool.

To make the syrup, put the water and the sugar into a saucepan along with the lemon rind and juice (photo 3), bring to the boil and simmer for 12 minutes. Strain and allow to cool before covering and freezing overnight.

Next morning, take the frozen syrup out of the freezer and place somewhere warm, as you want it to be quite sloppy when you come to finish the sorbet.

If you have a food processor, pour the sloppy basic stock syrup into the machine and add the apple purée. Switch on to high speed, add the egg white and then dribble in the double cream (photo 4). If you wish to leave out the double cream, use 3 egg whites at this stage. Pour the finished product into a suitable container, cover with cling film or a lid and freeze again.

If you do not have a food processor, beat the frozen syrup to a smooth paste, then whip in the purée, cream and stiffly whipped single egg white. If not using cream, beat the 3 egg whites to a stiff texture in a separate bowl and fold into the mix. Then freeze as above.

Sorbets need to be started the day before use and are best for eating immediately they have set on their second freezing. If kept for any length of time, they do tend to become slightly glassy and gritty; if this happens, I simply take the sorbet out of the freezer on the morning of the day I wish to serve it again, allow it to become soft, whizz it in the food processor once more and re-freeze.

AND TO DRINK

Some of the liqueur or booze you have used in the sorbet, chilled.

Elderflower sorbet

OTHER NATURE IS SUCH a splendid and generous provider, it is a great pity that so many of her efforts go to waste. Each June and July on my daily walks with my dog I collect enormous bunches of elderflowers and they are put to use at the hotel every other day. Succulent loins of pork are roasted on beds of them; flowers are scattered over plain baked fillets of sole or plaice; cooked gooseberries are enhanced by their flavour; elderflower sorbets top seasonal fruit salads; and gallons of elderflower wine are made to be served with summer puddings. At the farm I hang half a dozen large bunches of elderflowers to dry from the pine beams in the kitchen, and these enhance a winter fruit stock syrup or steamed sponge – quite apart from giving a wonderful homely look to the kitchen itself. If you are feeling a little off-colour, make a cup of dried elderflower tea or tisane: you will find it extremely soothing.

Towards autumn, in August and September, there are the elderberries, and these too are collected and used in gravies and sauces. A spoonful of home-made elderberry ketchup goes very well with cold lamb sandwiches, and handfuls of berries are often used in the apple and date chutney I love making at the end of each season.

Serve a portion of the following sorbet with some seasonal fruit, topped with a few mint leaves. It's very refreshing.

Serves 4

2 tablespoons lemon juice

finely grated rind of 1 lemon

1 pint (600 ml) water

6 oz (175 g) cane sugar

5 large elderflower heads, washed and dried

2 egg whites

Put everything except the egg whites into a clean saucepan and bring slowly to the boil. Remove from the heat and leave, covered, to cool. Strain off the flowers and put the syrup in a suitable dish, cover and freeze. When frozen, bring out into a warm kitchen and leave to become slushy. Beat the egg whites until stiff and fold into the sloppy syrup. Re-freeze.

Elderflower wine

I MAKE THIS in the plastic gallon containers in which our cream is delivered – your friendly supermarket should come to your assistance. Choose flower heads in full bloom, which are white. Avoid ones going creamy.

Makes just over 1 gallon (4.5 litres)

3 good handfuls elderflowers without leaves or stalks

1 gallon (4.5 litres) cold water

juice of 1 lemon

1 1/2 lb (700 g) caster sugar

2 tablespoons distilled white vinegar

Mix all the ingredients together, then divide between two clean containers. Secure the lids firmly and seal all around with sticky tape. Leave for 2–3 weeks in the coldest part of the house – or, better still, in the fridge. It all works to form a 'wine' with quite a bit of 'oomph'!

Home-made lemonade

*I*N THE SUMMER home-made lemonade is offered to tired travellers as they check in each afternoon at the hotel, and so I share this old-fashioned recipe with you. I often ring the changes by putting a head of elderflowers in the jug – but then the lemonade has to be strained before serving.

Makes about 1 pint (600 ml)

juice and finely grated rind of 3 lemons

juice and finely grated rind of 1 orange

4 oz (100 g) caster sugar

10 fl oz (300 ml) boiling water

Garnish

lemon slices and mint sprigs

Put the juice and rind of the lemons and orange into a large porcelain or earthenware jug (do not use an enamel one). Simply add the sugar, pour on the boiling water, and stir from time to time until cool. Put in the fridge to chill.

Serve with a few slices of lemon and a sprig of mint. I have also been known to garnish it with a few lightly scented rose petals!

Lemon ice-box pudding

*T*HIS IS A LIGHT, *tangy, refreshing pudding that can be made a few days ahead of time; in fact, you can keep it in the freezer without its losing flavour or texture for up to 2 weeks. You can also vary its flavours endlessly — lime, orange, soft fruits (but not pineapple).*

When you actually portion it, the pudding looks relatively uninspiring — just a rectangle of creamy-looking substance with three layers of sponge. Because of this I always serve it on old plates with a plain white centre but an extremely pretty decorated rim. You can also, of course, decorate the pudding itself, or the individual slices, as you wish; we used piped twirls of cream, tiny mint leaves and lemon segments.

Serves about 12

Sponge

3 oz (75 g) softened butter, plus extra for greasing

3 oz (75 g) caster sugar

1 large egg, lightly beaten

3 oz (75 g) self-raising flour, sifted

a little milk

Filling

2 eggs, separated

3 oz (75 g) caster sugar

finely grated rind of 2 lemons and the juice of 1 lemon

10 fl oz (300 ml) double cream

Pre-heat the oven to gas mark 4, 350°F (180°C), and smear the sides and base of a 2 lb (900 g) loaf tin (preferably a non-stick one) with a little butter.

Place the butter and sugar in a small mixing bowl and beat vigorously until light and fluffy. Add the egg little by little and fold in the flour. Add a little milk, if necessary, to achieve a dropping batter consistency. Pour into the prepared tin, knock it down gently and cook for 20 minutes in the pre-heated oven.

Remove the sponge from the oven, allow it to rest for a few minutes, then turn out on to a cooling rack. When it is completely cold, make two horizontal cuts to create three slices. Take care to ensure that the slices are of even thickness.

To make the filling, place the egg yolks in a small, warmed mixing bowl and whisk them — preferably using an electric hand beater — until they are light and fluffy. Then beat in the sugar little by little. This will

take you at least 8 minutes, even using the electric beater. Photo 1 compares the initial and finished textures.

Gently beat in the lemon rind and juice little by little. Transfer the mixture to a larger bowl. Beat the double cream until of a dropping consistency (photo 2) and combine this with the egg and sugar mix.

In another clean, dry bowl, beat the egg whites until stiff and 'peaking', and combine these with the filling mixture (photo 3).

In the bottom of the loaf tin in which you baked the sponge, place a sponge slice and spread it with half of the filling mixture (photo 4). Cover with a second slice of sponge, pour on the rest of the mixture, and top with the last slice of sponge. Cover with cling film, wrap in tinfoil and freeze for at least 24 hours.

About 30 minutes before serving, put the serving platter and individual plates in the fridge to chill well. Take the pudding out of the freezer and remove both tinfoil and cling film. Using a small palette knife dipped in very hot water, ease round the sides of the tin and turn the pudding out on to the chilled serving plate. At this stage, you can decorate it if you wish as described in the introduction to this recipe, cover again with cling film and return to the fridge.

To cut the pudding you need a serrated bread knife and a large jug of boiling water. Put the blade of the knife into the water, quickly cut a slice of pudding, pop the knife back into the water and repeat the process.

After the meal, any left-over pudding can be wrapped in cling film or tinfoil and put back in the freezer. If this sounds unhealthy, just ask yourself what happens to all the unsold cartons of ice-cream in the theatre or cinema when the lights go down, the salesgirl leaves the auditorium and the next act begins!

VARIATION

For a 'cowboy' version of this pudding you needn't bother to make the sponge. Simply line the loaf tin with a ¼ in (5 mm) thickness of crushed biscuits (ginger, shortbread or tea) mixed with a little softened butter, pour on the whole pudding mixture and top off with a similar crust of biscuits.

1 Little by little, beat the sugar into the egg yolks.

2 The double cream should be of a dropping consistency before you combine it with the egg and sugar mix.

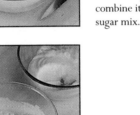

3 Beat the egg whites until stiff, then combine with the filling mix.

4 Place the bottom layer of sponge in the tin, then top with half the filling mixture.

St Clement's cheesecake

CHILLED CHEESECAKES were the rage in every host and hostess's culinary repertoire in the early sixties, but seemed to vanish from the scene thereafter. I, too, used to make them often at that time, and it wasn't until a few years ago that I happened to pull out my well-thumbed and rather tatty recipe. I'm glad to say cheesecakes have been on my home culinary menu ever since. I will continue to serve them until I am unable to cope in the kitchen: their texture is decadent; their taste can be differently delicious each time you make them; they are really easy to prepare, and will come to no harm if made 24 hours ahead of serving.

The following recipe is for a cheesecake which uses the juice and rind of both oranges and lemons (hence 'St Clement's). However, once you have made this and have grasped the technique, endless variations on the theme may be produced provided you use the same basic measures. (Everything remains the same except for the spirit used with the gelatine and the flavouring – here the orange and lemon rind and juice – folded into the basic mix. To make a coffee rum nut cheesecake, for instance, add flavouring of a couple of tablespoons of Camp coffee essence to the basic cheesecake, and reconstitute the gelatine with 3 tablespoons dark rum and 2 tablespoons water; fold in some chopped walnuts to the mix prior to pouring on to the biscuit base. Another variation is to fold raspberries into the basic mix, and use Pernod or Framboise with the gelatine.

Serves 8–10

Biscuit base

10 oz (275 g) chocolate digestive biscuits

2 oz (50 g) butter, melted

Cheesecake

½ oz (15 g) powdered gelatine (see step-by-step photos on p. 129)

3 tablespoons gin mixed with 2 tablespoons cold water

9 oz (250 g) good cream cheese

3 medium eggs, separated

2 oz (50 g) caster sugar

10 fl oz (300 ml) double cream

juice and finely grated rind of 1 lemon

finely grated rind of 3 oranges

Garnish

10 fl oz (300 ml) double cream

2 tablespoons icing or caster sugar

1 Press the biscuit crumb mixture firmly on to the lined base of the tin.

2 Only *half*-fill the piping bag with the whipped cream.

3 Squeeze the cream gently down to the base of the bag.

Pre-heat the oven to gas mark 4, 350°F (180°C), and line the base and sides of a 10 in (25 cm) loose-bottomed cake tin with thick greaseproof paper.

For the biscuit base, crush the biscuits in a liquidiser, dropping them in through the hole in the lid *one by one*. (Don't go putting the whole packet in and burning out the motor!) If you haven't got a liquidiser, break the biscuits up into tiny pieces, put them between two sheets of greaseproof paper and crush them into crumbs with a heavy rolling pin. Put the crumbs into a mixing bowl and bind together with the melted butter. Firmly press this mixture on to the lined base of the tin (photo 1). Bake in the pre-heated oven for 20 minutes, remove and allow to cool.

Now make the cheesecake. Put the gelatine into a small saucepan and in one fell swoop add the gin-and-water mix. Leave to one side.

In a bowl, cream the cheese, egg yolks and caster sugar together. In another bowl beat the double cream until it forms peaks, and then fold into the cheese mixture along with the lemon juice and lemon and orange rind. In yet another clean bowl beat the egg whites until stiff, then fold these into the mix.

Over a very gentle heat, reconstitute the gelatine and, when perfectly clear, pass through a fine sieve into the mix. Fold in very carefully and thoroughly. Pour into the prepared cake tin and leave in the fridge for 3–4 hours to set.

To prepare the garnish, whip the double cream to a peak consistency with the sugar. *Half*-fill a plastic piping bag with the whipped cream (photo 2) — never put more than this in, or you will have problems) — and gently squeeze the contents down to the base (photo 3). I find plastic piping bags the best and I always use plastic nozzles: the tin ones can cause horrific sores if they pierce your skin when being washed up. Hold the piping bag and slowly pipe twirls of cream on top of the cheesecake (see main photo). (You can practise this beforehand by using reconstituted dried potato!)

AND TO DRINK

The liqueur you used for the cheesecake, served frappé.

Meringues

MERINGUES, ALONG WITH PASTRIES, are most likely to give rise to SOS calls from the people who attend cookery courses. This always bewilders me as I find them among the easiest items to cook.

Once, on one of these courses, I had to suffer a home economist who, after every dish I demonstrated, said: 'Oh, is that *the way you do it?*' After watching me prepare a hazelnut meringue gâteau, she took me on one side and quietly pointed out all the technical faults. That evening I took her a plate of my gâteau — she was amazed!

So, in spite of the experts, here are my secrets for making good meringues. The eggs must be old and cold. The whites should always be weighed (photo 1). A metal bowl and beater should be used, and both should have been meticulously cleaned. Only the best greaseproof paper should be used: it's no use buying cheaper quality only to find that it sticks to the baking tray when heated.

These quantities are for 12 meringues which, when stuck together, will make six enormous portions (the size I like to serve to folk at the end of a three-course supper just to see their eyes pop!) — or they can make up to 20 small meringues.

Serves 6 generously

oil for greasing

6 oz (175 g) egg whites (you'll need 5 or more eggs)

12 oz (350 g) caster sugar, sifted

Filling

10 fl oz (300 ml) or more double cream

1 tablespoon caster sugar, sifted

1 tablespoon booze of your choice (optional)

Garnish

strips of red grapes

Pre-heat the oven to the very lowest gas mark possible, 200°F (100°C). Prepare two baking trays by lightly oiling the *undersides*: this way there is no block – i.e. the *lip* of the tray – between the heat and meringue

mix, and the oil ensures that the greaseproof paper doesn't slither about when the meringue mixture is being portioned on to it.

Whisk the carefully weighed egg whites for a few moments until they just start to froth and add the first dessertspoonful of sugar (photo 2). Continue to whisk and add the sugar spoonful by spoonful. Don't add too much sugar at a time or the meringue will never get off the ground.

It will take up to 10 minutes to beat in all the sugar (photo 3). I once read in an American women's magazine that the way to test whether the meringue mixture is ready is to invert the bowl over your head. The writer obviously had shares in a hairdressing firm – but she was right in indicating that it should be stiff enough to stay in the bowl!

Use two tablespoons to portion out the meringues on to the greaseproof paper-lined tray undersides (photo 4). Bake in the pre-heated oven for 4 hours, then turn off the heat and leave for a further hour with the oven door slightly open.

When the meringues are cool, store them in an air-tight container. They freeze well, but I always put them in the freezer in a tin to protect them in case some clot chucks a leg of lamb on top of them!

Be as generous as you like when it comes to the whipped cream filling, but 10 fl oz (300 ml) is the least you should use. When whipping it up, add 1 table-spoon of sifted caster sugar – and 1 tablespoon of booze if you feel like it. Use the cream to glue two baked meringues together to form one portion. In the main picture the meringues are finished with cream and garnished with strips of red grapes. Candied violets and rose petals also look nice – better than the usual glacé cherries and bits of angelica.

1 Always weigh the egg whites: for 6 oz (175 g) you will need about 5 eggs – perhaps more.

2 Add the caster sugar to the egg whites just 1 dessertspoon at a time.

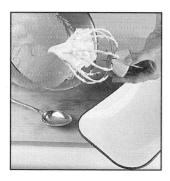

3 Beat the egg white and sugar for a good 10 minutes until glossy and stiff.

4 Spoon the meringue mix on to the lined *underside* of a baking tray to cook.

AND TO DRINK

The classic sweet dessert wine is, of course, Sauternes, but Muscat Beaumes de Venise is gentler on the pocket. It should be well chilled. If you come across it, consider the Australian Brown Brothers Milawa Estate Late-Picked Muscat Blanc.

Mousses

*M*OUSSES TAKE LITTLE *or no time to make and, because they are so light, little or no time to eat! Once the method has been followed several times you can play away to your heart's content experimenting with the basic flavouring.*

At the very mention of the word gelatine, some people's faces cloud over as, in previous attempts, their mixture has been half flabby and half-stiff, or full of hair-like strands. I always use powdered *gelatine, as it is available in sachets containing approximately* ¹/₂ *oz (15 g) — much more convenient than weighing out such a paltry amount yourself. As for leaf gelatine — forget it! Follow the instructions below and in the step-by-step photos, and gelatine will never be a problem again!*

Fills 12 × 3 in (7.5 cm) ramekins

¹/₂ oz (15 g) powdered gelatine

5 tablespoons liquid according to recipe (see opposite)

3 medium eggs, plus 2 egg yolks

2 oz (50 g) caster sugar, sifted

10 fl oz (300 ml) double cream

about 5 fl oz (150 ml) flavouring according to recipe (see opposite)

Garnish

whipped double cream

mint leaves

fruit

Whenever a recipe requires gelatine, always prepare it before you do anything else. Sprinkle the contents of the gelatine sachet on to the base of a small, clean saucepan. Then measure out separately the 5 tablespoons of liquid that are normally required. Pour these (photo 1) on to the gelatine in one go and gently shake until the gelatine dissolves. Put the pan to one side until you need to use it.

The mousse can be made using an electric hand whisk, but much better results are obtained from a larger mixer (not a food processor). A tip here is that the bowl and wire whisk must be very warm; I normally fill the bowl with boiling water and leave the whisk in for 5 minutes. Then pour away the water and dry the bowl and whisk well.

Put the eggs and egg yolks in the mixer bowl and beat away for a good 8–10 minute before you attempt to add any of the sugar. Then add the sugar very slowly, a spoonful at a time.

In a separate bowl lightly beat the double cream until it just starts to come together. Next, fold in the

1 Put the powdered gelatine in a small pan and pour the 5 tablespoons liquid on in one go.

2 Put the gelatine aside until it sets, or until ready to use it.

3 This is how the reconstituted gelatine should look.

4 Strain the liquid gelatine into the mousse mixture through a sieve, then fold in carefully.

chosen flavouring (see below). The mixture *has* to be floppy.

At this stage (photo 2), take the small saucepan of set gelatine and put it on the lowest heat possible. Allow the gelatine crystals to dissolve (photo 3).

Using a long-handled spoon fold the flavoured cream mixture into the egg and sugar mousse mix. Do this with infinite care, but at the same time make sure that both mixtures are well and truly combined. Now you need a very fine plastic or metal sieve; if you use a metal one and your kitchen is cold, always warm it thoroughly, otherwise some of the reconstituted gelatine will stick to it. Strain the dissolved gelatine through the sieve into the main mixture (photo 4). Again using the long-handled spoon, ensure that the mixture is well combined.

Pour the mix into a jug with a good pouring lip and then portion it into the ramekins. To add further bite I usually put a generous sprinkling of the liqueur used to reconstitute the gelatine in the base of the ramekins before filling. Cover the filled ramekins and put in the fridge for 6–8 hours. Decorate with whipped cream, mint leaves and appropriate fruit.

GRAPEFRUIT MOUSSE

Use 3 tablespoons Pernod and 2 tablespoons of water to reconstitute the gelatine. Use 5 fl oz (150 ml) frozen concentrated grapefruit juice, defrosted, as flavouring for the cream.

RASPBERRY OR STRAWBERRY MOUSSE

Use 3 tablespoons brandy or Kirsch and 2 tablespoons water to reconstitute the gelatine. Use about 5 fl oz (150 ml) puréed and sieved soft fruit to flavour the cream.

APPLE MOUSSE

Use 3 tablespoons Calvados and 2 tablespoons water to reconstitute the gelatine. Use about 5 fl oz (150 ml) sieved apple purée to flavour the cream.

ORANGE MOUSSE

Use 3 tablespoons orange-flavoured liqueur and 2 tablespoons water to reconstitute the gelatine. Use the finely grated rind of 2 oranges and 5 fl oz (150 ml) frozen concentrated orange juice, defrosted, as flavouring for the cream.

AND TO DRINK

The New World produces a few full-bodied rich Muscat wines which would be ideal with the mousses – or drink the spirit you used in them.

Chocolate coffee rum creams

YOU WILL HAVE GATHERED by now that most of the things I adore in life are 'bad for you' according to the experts. I take heart by remembering those who recommend that 'a little of what you fancy does you good'. (At least we will then smile and make others happy.) Moderation is the thing, I agree, but we should be able to splash out and enjoy ourselves once a week or so. Myself, I am a wine person: a few years ago when we were holidaying in an African game reserve, my friends bought me a carved white rhino with a card inscribed: 'To dear John, the Great White Wino'! Had they realised that my second passion is chocolate, what would they have bought?!

Chocolate was discovered by the Spaniards in Mexico in the early sixteenth century, and was used to make drinks — the name is derived from the Aztec word chocolatl *(choco meaning cocoa,* latl *meaning water). Nowadays few chocolates taste as they used to, and it's one of my hobby-horses. Many manufacturers seem to be interested only in the bottom line on the balance sheet instead of the end product on the production line. Never use milk chocolate or white chocolate for cooking, but go for a good dark chocolate made by a reliable maker — one you know and jolly well trust.*

Chocolate is not tricky to cook with as long as you remember the basic rule, which is that if it is melted over a direct high heat it will simply split, go gungy and be impossible to use. Always, but always, melt chocolate in a heatproof bowl set firmly over a pan of simmering water. Preferably add a little spirit to the chocolate to help it along and give it even

more 'oomph'. Never have the bowl submerged in water, and don't let the water boil either, as again the melting chocolate mixture could split.

This recipe is quite rich and should ideally be made about 6 hours before you wish to serve it, but it is just as good if made the evening before.

Fills 6 × 3 in (7.5 cm) ramekins

6 oz (175 g) good-quality plain chocolate, broken into pieces

1 oz (25 g) softened butter

2 tablespoons Camp coffee essence

3 tablespoons strong dark rum, plus a little extra (optional)

2 eggs, separated

5 fl oz (150 ml) double cream

pinch of free-running salt

Garnish

whipped double cream

chopped toasted hazelnuts

candied orange peel strips

1 Slowly melt the chocolate, butter, coffee essence and rum in a heatproof bowl set over simmering water.

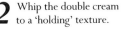

2 Whip the double cream to a 'holding' texture.

3 Combine the cream and chocolate mixture, using a long-handled spoon.

4 Divide the mix between the ramekins, then chill to set.

Place the broken-up chocolate, butter, coffee essence and rum into a heatproof bowl set over simmering water (photo 1) and leave until the ingredients are combined. Remove from the heat and beat in the egg yolks.

Whip the double cream to a 'holding' texture (photo 2) and gently combine the contents of both bowls, using a long-handled spoon or spatula (photo 3). Beat the egg whites and salt in a further clean bowl until very stiff and fold carefully into the mix.

Portion the mix into six ramekins (photo 4). To add a little extra to the dish you can splodge a little extra rum into each ramekin and spread it around the base and sides before adding the chocolate. Cover the dishes lightly with cling film – leave it comparatively loose, rather than too tight – and put in the fridge to set, which will usually take about 3–4 hours.

Garnish the chocolate creams with piped cream and perhaps a few chopped, toasted hazelnuts. A delicious further accompaniment would be the candied orange peel strips on p. 113.

AND TO DRINK

I would serve a Crème de Cacao frappé.

Chocolate ginger slice

I HEAR THAT ONE CAN *book chocoholic weekends for those partial to this delight, and one of these days I think I may well indulge in such an orgy. I have been known to use a little dark chocolate in an oxtail soup, and in a dark rich sauce to go with game. I find it terribly tempting not to select a double chocolate croissant when offered them for breakfast at some of the finer hotels on the Continent. When we were doing the photography sessions for this book, bars of chocolate were invariably produced when breaking point was nigh, and a personal indulgence is to have half a Wispa bar grated into a cup of hot rummy milk before bed. However, to combine the joyous luxury of chocolate with preserved ginger is, for me, the ultimate experience. To get the two flavours to blend completely, however, this slice has to be made at least the day — preferably a couple of days — before it is dished out to guests.*

You must cook only with the good, dark, unsweetened chocolate sold solely for cooking: this is the pure and unadulterated product of crushed cacao *(cocoa) beans. It is expensive, but if you decide to economise on your purchase, your end product will suffer. Cost-wise you might be aghast when you see the recipe needs 1 lb (450 g) of good dark chocolate and then 15 fl oz (450 ml) double cream — but in fact you will get twelve rich portions out of it! You can always consider starting* The BBC Diet *tomorrow!*

Serves 12

Crumb base

1 × 8 oz (225 g) packet chocolate digestive biscuits

2 oz (50 g) butter, melted, plus extra for greasing

Filling

2 oz (50 g) caster sugar

1 tablespoon syrup from the preserved ginger jar

2½ fl oz (65 ml) water

2½ oz (65 g) Chinese preserved stem ginger (about 5 nuggets), very finely chopped

1 lb (450 g) good-quality plain dark chocolate

4 tablespoons brandy

15 fl oz (450 ml) double cream

Garnish

sifted cocoa powder or whipped double cream and slivers of preserved stem ginger

Pre-heat the oven to gas mark 4, 350°F (180°C). Lightly grease a 10 in (25 cm) round, loose-bottomed cake tin and line the base and sides with a double thickness of good-quality greaseproof paper.

To make the base, crush, blend or liquidise the biscuits (if you do this using a machine, add the biscuits one at a time, not all at once). Combine the biscuit crumbs with the melted butter. Line the base of the prepared tin with this mixture and bake in the pre-heated oven for 20 minutes. Allow to cool.

To make the filling, put the caster sugar, syrup, water and stem ginger dice into a small saucepan, and gently bring to the boil, allowing the sugar to dissolve (photo 1). Put to one side.

Break up the chocolate, place in a large heatproof bowl with the brandy and put over a saucepan of simmering water (photo 2). The water should not boil and the base of the bowl should not touch the water. Allow the chocolate to melt, combining with the brandy (photo 3). Fold the cool sugar and syrup mix into the chocolate and leave to one side.

Whip the cream gently until it forms light peaks and combine with the chocolate mixture. Pour into the biscuit-lined tin (photo 4). Cover with cling film and leave in the fridge for at least 24 hours, preferably 48.

The dish can be decorated with sifted cocoa powder if you wish – never, *ever* use drinking chocolate, which contains a large amount of powdered milk – or simply piped with cream and decorated with slivers of preserved ginger.

1 Dissolve the sugar in the ginger syrup mix.

2 Place the chocolate and brandy in a bowl over simmering water.

3 Let the brandy combine with the melting chocolate.

4 Pour the chocolate mixture into the biscuit-lined tin.

AND TO DRINK

Crabbie's Green Ginger Wine on ice.

Sticky toffee pudding

I HOPE THIS INEXPENSIVE pudding will appeal to everybody — well, everybody who is not totally committed to watching every single calorie, and forever popping on and off the bathroom scales. It is simple to make, generous to serve (giving eight large to sixteen adequate portions), good for re-heating (particularly suitable, so I am told, for a microwave oven) and ideal for a Sunday lunch or simple supper party.

Walnut halves may be added to the mix, and 2 oz (50 g) of the flour could be replaced with ground hazelnuts. A smattering of sultanas can be scattered on the top as the pud goes into the oven — even better if these have been left to soak in cold tea or brandy overnight!

The ultimate indulgence is to double the quantity of the topping and, for sheer decadence, my adaptation of Delia Smith's butterscotch sauce makes the calorie count score the bull's eye; a diet the day after is the best prescription.

Serves 8–16

4 oz (100 g) softened butter, plus extra for greasing

6 oz (175 g) soft brown sugar

4 medium eggs, lightly beaten

8 oz (225 g) self-raising flour

1 teaspoon bicarbonate of soda

8 oz (225 g) stoned dates, finely chopped

2 tablespoons Camp coffee essence

10 fl oz (300 ml) boiling water

Topping

2 tablespoons double cream

3 oz (75 g) soft brown sugar

2 oz (50 g) butter

1 Line a square baking tin with a double thickness of greaseproof paper.

2 Combine the sponge ingredients, then pour the fairly runny mix into the lined tin.

3 When the pudding has been baked, pour over the sticky toffee topping.

Pre-heat the oven to gas mark 4, 350°F (180°C), and have ready a good, strong, leakproof, 9–10 in (23–25 cm) square tin. This should be lined with a double thickness of the best greaseproof paper (photo 1) and then painted with a little melted butter. Place this tin in a larger lipped tin for safety's sake – if you don't, when you pour the topping on, and the pud has shrunk slightly or the tin leaks, woe betide your kitchen! Using another tin ensures that the sauce will not wander.

Put the butter and sugar in a bowl and cream together. Take as much time as possible to do this – I find it best to start it off with the warmth of my hands, and then use the electric hand beater. Add the beaten eggs a little at a time.

Sift the flour and bicarbonate on to this mixture, then fold in until it resembles a sponge mix. Add the finely chopped dates. Mix the coffee essence and boiling water together and pour into the mixture, which will begin to bubble. At this stage the result will initially be wet and lumpy. Continue to mix using a big spoon and you will soon have this nice and smooth, but still rather runny (photo 2). Pour into the prepared tin set in its larger tin, place in the pre-heated oven and bake the pudding for 1½ hours.

Just before the pudding is ready, make the topping and the butterscotch sauce (see right). For the topping, simply combine the ingredients in a small saucepan and bring to the boil. When you take the cooked pudding out of the oven, pour the topping over it (photo 3), then brown under a hot grill. Serve the pudding cut into squares with a twirl of cream on the top if you like, and hand the sauce separately.

Butterscotch sauce

8 oz (225 g) golden syrup

2 oz (50 g) softened butter

2 oz (50 g) soft brown sugar

finely grated rind of 2 oranges

a few drops of vanilla essence

a little double cream (optional)

Put all the ingredients in a small saucepan and bring together over a low heat. If you are feeling totally decadent, beat in a couple of tablespoons of cream. The sauce is simplicity itself.

AND TO DRINK

To gild the lily, I would serve a glass of Frangelico, the Italian liqueur made from wild hazelnuts, with lots of crushed ice.

Boiled Lakeland loaf

*T*HIS IS AN OLD FAVOURITE, *and one that's easy to make. It is delicious served for tea if simply sliced and lavishly buttered; even better if toasted in front of the fire and spread with home-made rum butter. It also makes a delightful, if rather indulgent, bread and butter pudding.*

Use a standard cup holding 8 fl oz (250 ml) to measure the ingredients.

Makes 1 × 2 lb (1 kg) loaf

4 oz (100 g) softened butter, plus extra for greasing

1 cup cold water

1 cup sultanas or raisins

1 cup caster sugar

1 heaped teaspoon bicarbonate of soda

1 medium egg, lightly beaten

2 cups self-raising flour, sifted, plus extra for dusting

Pre-heat the oven to gas mark 3, 325°F (160°C), and grease and flour a 2 lb (900 g) loaf tin.

Put the butter, water, dried fruit and sugar into a deep saucepan, bring to the boil and simmer for 10 minutes. Remove from the heat and beat in the bicarbonate of soda – take care, as this often bubbles up like Mount Vesuvius. Leave to cool, then beat in the egg and stir in the flour.

Pour the runny mixture into the prepared tin (photo 1) and bake in the pre-heated oven for 1¼ hours. Turn out and leave to cool.

Rum butter

*Y*EARS AGO, WHITEHAVEN *became an important port, with rum and spices coming in from the Caribbean, and wool being exported. Now, every farm wife in Cumbria has her own version of this delicious recipe. I learned this particular one from my grandmother. The rum in those days was purchased by the measure from the local off-licence; as children we were always sent on this errand after dusk, so that the neighbours wouldn't cop on!*

The rum butter was used in bread and butter pudding – I offer my version opposite – for special occasions, and over the festive season my Nan would pop it under the lids of her hot, flaky, rich mince pies.

You can easily double up on the quantities given below if you want. I find it easiest to make the butter using an electric hand whisk and a warmed Pyrex bowl. Brandy can, of course, be substituted for the rum, making brandy butter!

Makes 8 oz (225 g)

4 oz (100 g) softened butter

4 oz (100 g) soft brown sugar

finely grated rind of 1 orange

½ nutmeg, finely grated

3 tablespoons dark rum

Cream together the butter and sugar until light and fluffy, beat in the orange rind and nutmeg and then, little by little, beat in the rum. Never add more liquid until the previous measure has 'disappeared'.

1 Pour the Lakeland loaf batter into the greased and floured loaf tin.

2 Slice the loaf very thinly for bread and butter pudding

3 Cut rounds from the loaf slices to fit the ramekins and butter them.

4 Top the ramekins up with the remaining cream and egg mixture just before cooking.

Bread and butter pudding

Serves 6

18 very thin slices Lakeland loaf (photo 2)

3 oz (75 g) rum butter (see opposite) or plain butter, plus extra for greasing

6 tablespoons sultanas, soaked overnight in 3 tablespoons booze (I usually use Van der Hum liqueur)

finely grated rind of 2 oranges

10 fl oz (300 ml) double cream

2 tablespoons caster sugar

2 medium eggs plus 1 egg yolk

grated nutmeg

Butter six ramekins. Cut the slices of loaf to fit the ramekins, using an appropriate round cutter, and butter each circle lightly (photo 3). Mix the sultanas with the orange rind and put ½ tablespoon in each ramekin. Follow this with another round of bread, a further ½ tablespoon sultanas and a third round of bread.

Beat the cream, sugar and eggs together, then divide most of this between the dishes. Leave to soak for at least 6 hours.

Pre-heat the oven to gas mark 5, 375°F (190°C) and, just prior to cooking, add the remaining cream and egg mixture to the ramekins (photo 4).

Place the ramekins in a roasting tin containing about 1 in (2.5 cm) of warm water and cook in the oven for 15–20 minutes. Remove and leave for 5 minutes before serving with some nutmeg grated over the top.

AND TO DRINK

Van der Hum liqueur on the rocks is the order of the day, but a well-chilled strong cider is also delicious.

Caramelised apple charlotte with coffee custard

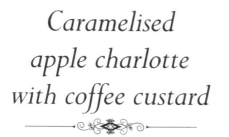

*I*N THE WINTER *departing dinner guests invariably have to venture out of a warm house into cold, frosty air. This baked apple charlotte leaves them well able to cope with the icy rigours of the night!*

The sponge mix and apples may be made 2–3 hours ahead of the actual cooking time. But the actual dividing up into individual ramekins must be done just before cooking. The unusual custard, too, can be made in advance and left covered with cling film.

Serves 6

2 oz (50 g) softened butter

2 tablespoons demerara sugar

2 tablespoons cider vinegar or white vinegar

2 lb (900 g) Granny Smith or other apples, peeled, cored and thinly sliced

Sponge

4 oz (100 g) softened butter, plus extra for greasing

4 oz (100 g) caster sugar

2 medium eggs

4 oz (100 g) self-raising flour, plus extra for dusting

Coffee custard

10 fl oz (300 ml) single cream

10 fl oz (300 ml) milk

8 egg yolks

2 oz (50 g) caster sugar

generous pinch of freshly ground nutmeg

1 tablespoon Camp coffee essence

Pre-heat the oven to gas mark 4, 350°F (180°C).

For the apples, put the butter and sugar into a thick-bottomed saucepan and bring them together over a gentle heat. Then turn up the heat a little and, stirring from time to time with a wooden spoon, let the mixture come to a dark-coloured 'bubble' stage. Add the vinegar, drop in the apples and turn them

occasionally over the heat for about 15 minutes: do not allow them to disintegrate. Transfer to a cold dish and allow to cool completely. Never use immediately, otherwise the sponge will be soggy in texture.

For the sponge, place the butter in a warm bowl, add the caster sugar and, preferably using an electric hand beater, beat for several minutes until the mix is white and fluffy. At this stage it cannot be overbeaten!

Lightly beat the eggs in another bowl and then beat them little by little into the butter and sugar mix. If you rush this, the mix will curdle, but don't throw it out if it does (photo 1 shows a good mix and a curdled one). Should this happen, stop using the beater, fold in 1 tablespoon flour, add a little more egg, and repeat until all the ingredients are used up.

If you have been clever enough not to curdle your mix, when all the egg has been incorporated, sift the self-raising flour into the bowl and gently fold it in. Use a large spoon with a long handle, which mustn't be held as if you are going to do battle – hold it gently.

Lightly grease six ramekins with butter. Put 1 teaspoon flour in the bottom of each one and roll it over the base and up the sides, tipping out any excess.

Divide two-thirds of the sponge mix between the ramekins and bring the mix slightly up the sides before adding the cooked apple (photo 2). Spread the rest of the sponge mix over the top. Place the ramekins in a roasting tin with 1 in (2.5 cm) of warm water in the base and bake in the pre-heated oven for 20 minutes.

Meanwhile, make the coffee custard. In a thick bottomed saucepan warm the cream and milk but do not allow to boil. In a small bowl cream the egg yolks with the sugar, nutmeg and coffee essence. Pour the cream and milk mixture on to this and beat thoroughly. Return to the saucepan and over a very low heat stir continuously until the custard coats the back of a wooden spoon (photo 3).

Take the cooked charlottes out of the oven and leave for about 3 minutes. Line a warmed serving plate with some coffee custard and, running a small knife around the ramekins to release the mix, turn the charlottes out on to the custard. Serve with more custard in a jug (main photo).

1 Mix the eggs *slowly* into the butter and sugar mix, otherwise the mix will curdle (as in the top bowl).

2 Layer the ramekins with sponge mix, apple, and more sponge mix on top.

3 Cook the coffee custard (or any custard) until it coats the back of a wooden spoon, and a finger trail stays.

AND TO DRINK

I suggest that you stay with the apple theme – a tot of Calvados or a glass of strong cider.

Old-fashioned custard

*M*EMORIES OF WARTIME *fare or school dinners might have given many people an aversion to custard, but there is nothing nicer with most hot puds than the recipe below. Once you have mastered it, you will never again resort to tins or packets. Those of you who have been put off in the past because your custard goes lumpy or splits will be saved both of these disasters because the cornflour acts as a stabiliser.*

Makes 1 pint (600 ml)

6 egg yolks

2 tablespoons caster sugar

2 level teaspoons cornflour

2 tablespoons cooking brandy (optional)

10 fl oz (300 ml) double cream

10 fl oz (300 ml) single cream

Place the egg yolks, sugar, cornflour and brandy in a large bowl. Beat them until smooth.

In a thick-bottomed saucepan large enough to hold all the ingredients comfortably, mix the two creams and bring them to the boil. Keep your eyes on the pan – if you turn your back, the cream will boil over!

Pour the cream on to the other ingredients and beat well together. Turn down the heat, return the mixture to the saucepan and then, stirring constantly with a wooden spoon, cook until the custard starts to thicken. Be sure not to overcook. When it is ready, the mixture should coat the back of the wooden spoon.

If you are not too happy about the texture of the custard, pass the mix through a fine sieve. Serve hot with a pudding like the upside-down sponge right, or leave to get cold and use in trifles like my Nan's tipsy trifle or serve with stewed fruit. You'll find the flavour of real old-fashioned custard transforms these traditional puddings.

Upside-down pineapple ginger hazelnut sponge

I PREFER TO USE *the old-fashioned rectangular 'tin' or enamel dish for this pudding, but of course a Pyrex dish can be used instead. It should measure 9 ×6 in (23 × 15 cm).*

Serves 6

½ oz (15 g) butter

1 oz (25 g) soft light brown sugar

2 thick slices fresh pineapple, halved and marinated overnight in 2 tablespoons green ginger wine

Sponge

3 oz (75 g) softened butter

3 oz (75 g) caster sugar

1 medium egg

3 oz (75 g) self-raising flour

2 oz (50 g) hazelnuts, toasted and coarsely chopped

On top of the stove, melt the butter and brown sugar in the pudding tin until they slightly caramelise, and then cook the pineapple slices in the mixture until brown (photo 1). Leave the slices in the tin. Pre-heat the oven to gas mark 4, 350°F (180°C).

Prepare the sponge mix according to the instructions on p. 154, fold in the toasted chopped hazelnuts, then spread on top of the pineapple in the tin. Bake in the pre-heated oven for 40 minutes. Place a warmed serving dish on top of the pudding and invert, so that it slides out upside-down (photo 2 and main photo).

My Nan's tipsy trifle

Make this in individual tall glasses, as shown in the main photo. For each trifle you need 2 oz (50 g) baked sponge which has been split, lined with cream and jam and cubed (see p. 155 and photo 3); put the cubes in the glass, and pour over 1 tablespoon sherry or Marsala, ½ tablespoon cooking brandy and 2 tablespoons apricot purée (photo 4). If making the purée with tinned apricots, use only the fruit, draining off the syrup. Top with 4 tablespoons cold custard and decorate if you like with a whirl of whipped cream and a cherry.

1 Brown the pineapple slices with butter and sugar in the pudding tin.

2 Place a warmed serving plate on top of the pudding, then invert so that the pudding slides out.

3 For the trifle, cut the jammed and creamed sponge into cubes.

4 Top the alcohol-topped cubes with apricot purée.

AND TO DRINK

I wouldn't serve anything with the pineapple pudding, but the trifle could take a nice glass of chilled sherry or Madeira.

Junket

I WAS SIX WHEN WAR broke out, and living in Barrow-in-Furness. Rationing, introduced in January 1940 and lasting until 1954, affected all my early years and food lore. At first we had just 12 oz (350 g) sugar and 4 oz (100 g) butter and bacon per person per week. An allowance of 1 lb (450 g) meat and restrictions on tea, margarine and cheese followed soon after. There was immediately a thriving black market in food, so in December 1941 a fair system of food points was introduced.

Food was terribly important as part of the battle on the home front, and it has been said that in wartime we were healthier as a nation, thanks to the well-balanced, rationed diet. The government, quite rightly, decided that they could accurately judge what people basically needed to eat in order to live. My memory, even from the age of eight, is that we were never craftier in making the best of what we had or what we could get our hands on. Swapping, bartering and getting a little of this and that on the side was rife. Our weekly walk and visit to the cemetery was extended, for instance, to take in local woods, where the elderberries, sloes, cobnuts, crab apples, hip-haws and other wild berries were collected. Seasonal bottling became the talking point of all and sundry as each household Kilner-jarred its way through food such as plums and tomatoes.

Shopping was a nightmare, and queueing became an obsession. People would join a queue, then ask the person in front what they were queuing for. I remember once joining one in the market, having been told chips were on sale. I was totally bewildered when it was my turn to be served to be confronted by a real spiv selling zips. I bought four, and my Nan was dead chuffed!

Some of the dishes made during the war years sound unbelievable today, but I can remember them all. Left-over porridge was mixed with breadcrumbs, formed into cakes and fried in bacon fat. Tapioca was used for thickening jams made with honey because sugar was short. My Nan got to never telling any of us what a dish was made of until we had tasted it – and, more important still, liked it. One dish that the family could never take to was whalemeat steaks, which came on to the market in 1945. I can smell them now being cooked in the small kitchen, and my hair stands on end.

Mayonnaise was made from custard and milk powders, with mustard, margarine, vinegar and boiling water. One very small tin of pineapple chunks would be turned into a salad for six with mountains of lettuce. Two small chunks of pineapple (at the most) per person, covered in grated cheese, was the highlight of a Sunday high tea.

I got a job in our school canteen on the dishwashing machine during the lunch hour, and soon learned to get all the scrapings from the side of the roast trays, and to wangle a bit of extra pudding from Mrs Frost, the senior cook. Then I spent my 2s 1d (10½p) weekly dinner money on cream buns, Horlicks and Ovaltine tablets on the way home from school. No wonder I was a fat, spotty devil, and, with such basic training, no wonder I still love my food.

One thing our family never seemed to be short of during rationing, though, was milk. We used it for endless puddings like tapioca, semolina, blancmange – and junket. In the war years my Nan made it using Benger's Junket Powders, and I can remember to this day her rage when the sweetening was taken out and we had to use our precious sugar ration instead. I still love this dish and serve it with home-made biscuits (see p. 160).

Today rennet for making junket can be bought at good delicatessens. It has to be fresh, and once opened it has a short shelf-life.

Serves 6

1 pint (600 ml) fresh milk

4 teaspoons caster sugar

2 teaspoons Camp coffee essence

½ teaspoon rennet

All you do is bring the milk, sugar and coffee essence to blood temperature over a low heat. (I must admit I stir it with my fingers.) Add the rennet and pour into a dish. It will set in about 5 minutes.

AND TO DRINK

What else, to try to recreate the period, but a glass of home-made elderflower wine (see p. 121)

Rough puff pastry

PUFF PASTRY HAS MANY USES in everyday cooking and party catering, but so often I hear people say that they can't be bothered to make it when perfectly good frozen pastry can be bought so easily. I think that this is just an, excuse, perhaps from those who have tried the 'classic' technique and become bored by the length of the process or bewildered by the method. I must admit I cannot, for the life of me, make the truly classical puff where the big blob of butter is placed in the middle and you roll it into the dough! I must have tried dozens of times, and always given up in sheer frustration. Even when I've made it through to the end, my interpretation isn't a patch on the following rough puff pastry, which we use all the time at Miller Howe. The old wives' tale of the need for very cold hands, a cold slab and warm heart is about as true as declaring that I will be the next 007! The staff and I have made this all round the world, in all kinds of kitchens, under all sorts of conditions, and it always turns out the same.

If I've enthused you, please do read the following points two or three times so that you are aware of certain potential pitfalls.

1 Strong plain flour is a must.

2 The margarine and lard must be **really** soft.

3 The lemon juice must be freshly squeezed.

4 The water must be icy cold. When I put out the fats to soften, I also measure the water into a large jug and put in as many ice cubes as possible. I then return the water to the fridge and measure the quantity again just before using.

5 You need a 4–5 in (10–13 cm) soft-bristled paintbrush.

6 A strong wooden rolling pin and a large plastic bowl are also required.

Most recipes call for 30 minutes rest between stages, but I find that the pastry doesn't need anything like this. In fact, if you make two batches at a time, while you complete a stage on one batch the other batch will rest sufficiently. The following quantities are for one mix only; if doing just one, allow a 5-minute break between each stage.

Makes 2½ lb (1.1 kg)

1 lb (450 g) strong plain flour

generous pinch of free-running salt

8 oz (225 g) soft margarine (the spread-from-the-fridge type is fine)

8 oz (225 g) soft vegetable shortening or lard

1 tablespoon fresh lemon juice made up to 10 fl oz (300 ml) with ice-cold water

Sift the flour and salt into a large mixing bowl and scatter over them the two fats, broken into walnut-sized lumps. Coat the fat lumps very gently with flour but do not squeeze or press.

Make a small hollow in the middle of the mixture to

take the liquid, add it, and, using a palette knife (preferably) or long-handled spoon, combine to a rough dough. Turn this out on to a well-floured work surface (photo 1).

As gently as possible, shape the dough into a brick shape and, using a rolling pin, make indentations in the middle, top and bottom (photo 2). Sprinkle with flour if large areas of fat are visible. Gently place the rolling pin in the middle depression and carefully and patiently roll the 'top' part of the brick away from you; never let the rolling pin come back hard towards you. Repeat from the bottom indentation towards the middle. You want to get a perfect rectangle after each roll. It is important to have square corners; avoid an oval of pastry like the one shown in photo 3.

Brush off any surplus flour with a soft-bristled paintbrush kept specially for the purpose, and fold the bottom third of the pastry up and away from you over the middle third; bring the top third down over this (photo 3). After the rolling and folding process, press down gently with the rolling pin on the three 'open' sides (photo 4) and allow to rest for 5 minutes (or while you deal with the other batch of pastry if making two simultaneously).

Flour the work surface and, if necessary, also sprinkle flour over the pastry, brushing off any surplus. Repeat the rolling and folding three more times; each time give the pastry a quarter-turn, from 12 noon to 3 o'clock! Never stretch the pastry.

After the fourth turn, the dough should be light and springy. Put it into a plastic bag and chill in the fridge if you intend using it on the same day; put it in the freezer if you wish to store it. In either case it must always return to room temperature before use.

Use the puff pastry to make squares, rounds, vol-au-vents, cornets, straws and so on. These should be chilled after rolling and cutting, then egg-washed before going into a very hot oven at gas mark 8–9, 450–475°F (230–240°C). Cook until golden to dark brown.

1 Turn the rough dough on to a well-floured work surface. The fat lumps are very clearly visible.

2 Shape into a brick shape, then make three indentations with the rolling pin.

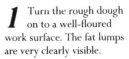

3 Roll into a long rectangle (not oval as on the left), then fold the bottom third up, and the top third down over this.

4 Press down gently with the rolling pin on the three 'open' sides.

Savoury pastry tarts

Y*EARS AGO MY FRIEND Margaret Costa wrote about my pastries in the Sunday Times. She stated that wives, mothers and lovers often feel a total sense of frustration when serving soggy or hard, indifferent pastries, but she went on to say that if they followed my recipes their love life should improve! I know nothing about this. But I do know that the actual pastry is so easy to make, store, cook and serve.*

The staff and I have made up to 450 lb (200 kg) of pastry for our annual winter tour to the United States and other countries. The whole load is deep-frozen, packed into deep-freeze containers and then into large metal theatrical trunks, flown across the Atlantic in the aircraft's hold and immediately transferred to freezers or fridges when we arrive at each city hotel. At the end of three and a half weeks the last ball of pastry is as good as the first. What better proof do you need that pastry is easy?

The pastry recipe makes enough for three 8–10 in (20–25 cm) quiches; the filling here is for one quiche, to serve eight first-course portions.

Pastry

1 lb (450 g) plain flour

pinch of salt

2 tablespoons fine icing sugar

10 oz (275 g) softened butter

2 medium eggs, at room temperature

Quiche custard

10 fl oz (300 ml) double cream

2 eggs plus 1 egg yolk

pinch of salt

freshly ground black pepper

pinch of grated nutmeg

Filling

about 12 oz (350 g) ingredient(s) of your choice (see right)

1 Sift the flour, salt and icing sugar on to the work surface and make a well in the middle.

2 Press the softened butter into this well, leaving visible impressions which will 'hold' the egg yolks.

3 When the eggs and butter look like scrambled eggs, start incorporating the flour using the length of the palette knife at a 90-degree angle.

4 Chill the pastry well in a plastic bag before rolling.

should form into small round crumbs, then 'sultanas', then walnut-sized pieces; and when all the areas of flour have vanished, simply divide the dough into three. Roll carefully into three balls, wrap in a plastic bag (photo 4) and chill.

Line a fluted, loose-bottomed flan tin using one portion of the pastry, then line with tinfoil and chill again. While the pastry is chilling, pre-heat the oven to gas mark 3, 325°F (160°C).

Fill the pastry case with ceramic baking beans, rice or dried peas and bake blind in the pre-heated oven for 40 minutes. Make sure when you remove it from the oven and take out the tinfoil that the base is completely dry. Turn the oven up to gas mark 5, 375°F (190°C).

Simply beat all the quiche custard ingredients together and use in conjunction with your chosen filling – the one shown in the main picture is broad bean and red pepper. Other possibilities are sautéed onions or mushrooms, onions and bacon, smoked trout and mushrooms, smoked salmon (soaked beforehand in some milk), and broccoli with cheese or bacon. Pour into the pastry case and bake in the oven for approximately 35 minutes. Serve warm as a starter, cut into eight wedges.

When making pastry, get into the habit of sifting the flour mixed with the salt and icing sugar on to the work surface. Make a well in the middle of the flour (photo 1), put in the very soft butter and press down, leaving visible thumbprints that will hold the yolks as you break the eggs on to it, which you should now do (photo 2).

With your fingertips tap away at the egg and butter mix until it resembles scrambled eggs, but take care not to incorporate too much of the surrounding flour. When the mix looks as it does in photo 3, use a long palette knife to flick the flour all over the butter mix and start to incorporate the flour with the butter as shown. It is essential that your palette knife goes through at 90 degrees and that you do not press it flat as this will make the final pastry heavy. The mixture

AND TO DRINK

The Torres Gran Vina Sol Reserva from Spain is a very proud wine to serve with practically any quiche – but go for the Sauvignon grape, preferably matured in heavy oak.

Farmhouse pastry soured apple pie

*T*HIS VERY RICH PASTRY *has a hundred and one purposes at the hotel, but is always used for good old-fashioned farmhouse pies (see also p. 184/185). I used it recently on one of our cooking trips to New York to make a pear, walnut and Stilton pie which was a great hit. You can vary the filling as much as you like so long as you follow my pastry-making instructions. The filling here is actually the result of an idea we picked up from the Union League Club where we cook when in New York.*

There are a few important points to bear in mind when preparing farmhouse pastry. It is always best to make it in a very large bowl which has a rounded rather than flat bottom — like the one in the small photos. I also mean it when I continually say that you have to be in the mood for doing this dish: a light heart truly does mean a light hand and thus light pastry! The ingredients must be accurately *weighed out, preferably on the old-fashioned balancing scales which have a pan on one side and a ledge for weights on the other. The butter should be nice and soft so that when you press your thumb in, the impression remains very clearly. The flour and cornflour must be sifted.*

These ingredients will be sufficient to line a 10 in (25 cm) fluted flan tin approximately 2 in (15 cm) deep. If the one you have is only 1 in (2.5 cm) deep, halve the filling and reduce the cooking time accordingly.

Serves about 8

Farmhouse pastry

6 oz (175 g) self-raising flour

1 oz (25 g) cornflour

6 oz (175 g) softened butter

2 oz (50 g) caster sugar

finely grated rind of ½ lemon

1 large egg, lightly beaten

Filling

2 lb (900 g) Granny Smith apples

2 eggs

4 oz (100 g) soft brown sugar

2 oz (50 g) self-raising flour

10 fl oz (300 ml) soured cream

Topping

2 oz (50 g) self-raising flour

1 oz (25 g) demerara sugar

4 oz (100 g) pecan nuts or walnuts

3 oz (75 g) soft butter

pinch each of ground nutmeg, ginger and cinnamon

To make the pastry, sift the flour and cornflour into a round-bottomed mixing bowl. Break the soft butter up into about eight pieces and scatter these on the flour. Now stand away from the bowl and hold your two hands palm upwards across your stomach (photo 1) with the fingers slightly apart. Holding your fingers *still*, waggle your thumbs up and down. Just as for the savoury cheese pastry in the next recipe, these are the movements you employ when you put your hands into the flour and butter. Bring your hands up above the bowl, gently easing the butter in and allowing it to drop back into the bowl (photo 2). You must *not* be uptight and stiff – relax and enjoy the job. You will soon develop a lovely co-ordinated movement, and the mixture will begin to feel wet. Do not overwork it, though.

When the flour has all vanished into the fat, sprinkle on the sugar and lemon rind and very, very gently combine. Zig-zag the beaten egg over the mixture (photo 3) then, holding the rim of the bowl in each hand, swirl it round as if you are panning for gold, lightly throwing the mix up (photo 4). It will soon start to form lumps, then, very gently, you bring it together using the palm of your hand. If your kitchen and hands are cold, you might need to add 1 tablespoon of water to help bind the dough, which should be soft in texture. Put it in a plastic bag and leave in the fridge overnight.

The next day roll out the pastry only when it has come round to that same soft texture in your warm kitchen. Line the base and sides of a 10 in (25 cm) fluted flan tin, 2 in (5 cm) in depth, with the pastry (see p. 151 for details) and chill again.

Pre-heat the oven to gas mark 3, 325°F (160°C). Line the pastry in the tin with tinfoil and ceramic baking beans and bake blind in the oven for 30–40 minutes or until crisp and dry. Remove from the oven and take out the beans and tinfoil (carefully as, being such a rich pastry, it can stick to the foil). You might need a slightly longer cooking time if the pastry is not crisp and dry enough: put back in the oven for 5–10 minutes to make doubly sure that it is well cooked. There is nothing worse than a pie with a soggy bottom!

Leave the pie base to cool while you make the filling. Raise the temperature of the oven to gas mark 4, 350°F (180°C). Peel, core and thinly slice the apples and then put a covering of them on the base of the cooled cooked pie base. Mix the eggs, sugar and

self-raising flour into the soured cream and pour a little of this over the apples. Build up alternate layers until you have used all the ingredients. Bake in the oven for 40 minutes.

Meanwhile, make the topping by simply mixing together the topping ingredients in a food processor.

Remove the pie from the oven and turn the temperature up yet again to gas mark 6, 400°F (200°C). Scatter the topping over the partly cooked pie, then bake for a further 15 minutes. Remove from the oven and leave for at least 15 minutes before serving.

1 Scatter the pieces of butter on the flour, then hold your hands in front of you, palms upwards and fingers slightly apart.

2 Ease the butter into the flour above the bowl, using spread fingers and a light thumb 'waggle' across them.

3 Zig-zag the beaten egg over the mixture in the bowl.

4 Swirl the bowl around and up until the mixture gradually comes together.

AND TO DRINK

Some wonderful Calvados from Normandy.

Apple pie with savoury cheese pastry

*T*HERE IS AN OLD *North Country saying that goes: 'Apple pie without a cheese is like a kiss without the squeeze.' Here is a version of my Nan's cheese pastry which she used for apple pies way back in the thirties. They were baked on deep, blue-rimmed, tin plates and then piled into an enormous wicker basket that she would hump down to the local shipyard in time for the noon lunch-break buzzer. The wares she sold also included meat and potato pasties, fly cakes, savoury tea-cakes filled with her own brawn, and meat loaf accompanied by pickled onions and chutneys. She would wait for the men to finish their meal, pack the empty dirty containers in her basket, and on the way home fill this with washing from two ladies for whom she 'did'. The boiler in the wash-house was in use during the afternoon for this chore, and then cleaned out; it was often used early in the evening for boiling hams and joints of mutton. This boiler was fuelled by coal and wood and needed constant attention, particularly as regards the quality of the kindling. I remember one day her telling me*

to call in at the coalman in the next back-street to ask for two bags of coal to be delivered next morning without fail. For years I thought 'coal without fail' was a special type mined for my Nan!

Makes 1 × 10 in (25 cm) pie

about 1¼ lb (550 g) apples

finely grated orange rind

soft brown sugar

1oz (25 g) strong Cheddar cheese, finely grated

Savoury cheese pastry

4 oz (100 g) self-raising flour, sifted

4 oz (100 g) wholemeal flour

generous pinch of salt

4 oz (100 g) very soft butter

2 oz (50 g) strong Cheddar cheese, finely grated

1 egg, lightly beaten

1 tablespoon cold water

Make the pastry first. Put the two flours and the salt into a large bowl and combine. It is absolutely essential that the butter is nice and soft: break it up into walnut-sized lumps and scatter over the flours. Then scatter the cheese in as well and rub it and the butter into the flours exactly as described for the farmhouse pastry on p. 149. Lightly mix the beaten egg with the cold water and pour this over the mix. Using your working hand only, with fingers widely apart, keep scooping up the flour and butter mix and gently 'persuade' the egg and water into it to form a dough. Divide the mix in half and coax each half into a ball. Wrap in tinfoil, cling film or greaseproof paper, remembering exactly how soft it feels, and chill.

The pie base must not be rolled until the pastry has 'come back' to this stage. To line the base of a 10 in (25 cm) loose-bottomed flan tin, remove it from the tin, place it on the work surface and scatter flour round the outside edge (photo 1). Put a ball of pastry on the base and gently, from the middle, roll it until it goes beyond the perimeter of the base and on to the flour in sufficient quantity to come up the pie sides (photo 2). Bring this outside 'rim' of pastry back over on to the base with a palette knife and, by sliding the knife under the base, lift it and the pastry into the tin (photo 3). It is then a simple task to ease the pastry up the sides of the tin and level it off around the rim. Chill in the fridge.

When you are ready to cook, pre-heat the oven to gas mark 3, 325°F (160°C). Line the pastry case with tinfoil, weight with ceramic baking beans and bake blind in the pre-heated oven for 30–40 minutes or until nice and dry. Remove the foil and the beans and allow to cool.

Peel, core and thinly slice the apples (you should have about 1 lb/450 g left in weight after preparation) and mix with plenty of grated orange rind. Scatter a little sugar on the base of the cooled pastry case, fill with the apple slices, then add more sugar. Roll out the second ball of pastry to form a lid for the pie. Flop it over the rolling pin and then over the top of the apples (photo 4). Seal well and neaten, and bake in the oven at gas mark 4, 350°F (180°C), for 40–45 minutes. As the pie comes out of the oven, scatter the remaining grated cheese on top.

1 Chill the pastry, then return to its original temperature and texture before rolling. Place on the removable base of the flan tin and flour *around* the base.

2 Gently roll the pastry beyond the edge of the flan tin base, allowing enough to form the eventual sides of the flan.

3 Flop these sides over into the centre and place the prepared pastry on base in its fluted tin. Ease the pastry from the middle up the sides of the tin.

4 Fill the blind-baked flan case with apples, then roll out the pie lid and flop on to the pie from a rolling pin.

AND TO DRINK

Once again, chilled Calvados.

Hazelnut galettes with caramelised apples

I *AM, TO SAY THE LEAST*, nuts about nuts, and my favourite is the hazelnut. If, like me, you tend to buy nuts in the shell for Christmas, and never get around to using them up, then this is a good time to make this pastry. But, as with most good things, there are good and bad nuts. It is often best to pay that little bit extra at your local health-food shop than spend a few pence less at the supermarket. The most common hazelnut bought in this country is imported from Spain – the large, broad variety which is thick-shelled, reddish-brown in colour and quite sweet.

This recipe calls for ground hazelnuts which can, I know, be bought quite easily ready-prepared, but it is so much cheaper and better to grind your own at home if you have a food processor or liquidiser. Simply spread the shelled nuts on a baking tray and put in a warm oven at gas mark 2, 300°F (150°C), for about 15 minutes. Wearing an old pair of woollen gloves to protect your fingers, take a handful of nuts and rub them vigorously together, letting the skins drop off on to a sheet of newspaper. Don't let the warm nuts go cold or else the skin will be impossible to remove. There are those who insist on painstakingly removing every last scrap of dark skin, but I don't agree; there is flavour in the skin, so leave any bits that are proving difficult to get off. Grind the skinned nuts in your liquidiser or processor, but don't put a whole 1 lb (450 g) in at one go. Drop them in a handful at a time and allow the machine to do the job without straining the motor. Make absolutely sure that some of the nuts haven't evaded the blades before using them.

The following pastry recipe makes double the quantity required, so chill or freeze the second half for use another day.

Of course, the basic 'galette' biscuits are delicious just as

they are, with morning coffee, or you could stick them together in pairs with a coffee-flavoured butter cream. The basic pastry recipe can be baked blind in a loose-bottomed flan tin with the apple mixture added when the pastry is cold. The permutations are almost endless . . .

Serves 4

Hazelnut galette pastry

6 oz (175 g) softened butter

4 tablespoons caster sugar

8 oz (225 g) plain flour

6 oz (175 g) ground hazelnuts

Caramelised apples

4 oz (100 g) softened butter

4 oz (100 g) soft brown sugar

6 large Granny Smith apples, peeled, cored and coarsely sliced

To serve

5 fl oz (150 ml) double cream, whipped

icing sugar

For the pastry, beat the butter and sugar together until very light, fluffy and creamy. Fold in the flour and ground hazelnuts. Divide the mixture into two balls, place in plastic bags and chill well in the fridge. Remove one ball only for this recipe, and let it return to room temperature before rolling.

Pre-heat the oven to gas mark 4, 350°F (180°C), and have ready a baking tray lined with greaseproof paper. Roll out the pastry on a floured surface to a thickness of just under ¼ in (5 mm) and cut into 12 × 3 in (7.5 cm) circles. Transfer to the prepared baking tray and bake in the pre-heated oven for 10 minutes. Cool on a rack.

To make the caramelised apples, melt the butter, add the sugar and then the apples (photo 1). Using a wooden spoon to turn the mixture from time to time, cook gently until the apples are brown and toffee-like (photo 2).

When you are ready to assemble the biscuits and apple, you will need three rounds of biscuits for each portion, with two layers of cold apple filling. For extra luxury, pipe whipped double cream round the edge of the lower and middle biscuit layers before filling with apple (photo 3). Crown with the third biscuit and dust the top with icing sugar (photo 4).

1 Add the sugar and sliced apples to the melted butter.

2 Cook gently until the apples are brown and toffee-like – when they have caramelised.

3 To assemble the galettes, pipe whipped cream around the outside of two rounds, and fill both with caramelised apple.

4 Top the two apple and cream layers with a third biscuit and dust with icing sugar.

AND TO DRINK

An orange-flavoured, chilled liqueur.

Victoria sponges

O N COOKERY COURSES one often hears from ladies — obviously good cooks — that their sponges split, are heavy or sink. I do find this very hard to understand. The basic method used is virtually that for any creamed cake, and the variations are never-ending. I can vividly recall my grand-mother making the following recipe in a large yellow pot, patterned on the outside but looking like a spider's web on the once-white inside, with the odd chip or two round the rim. She used her rheumatic hand to cream the butter and sugar and then, with the same hand, beat in the egg little by little at a mind-boggling speed.

Nowadays I always use a large plastic bowl and an electric whisk which makes light work of the job. The basic sponge cakes keep extremely well if stored in air-tight plastic bags after they have been left to get quite cold, or they can be frozen.

Makes 4 × 7 in (18 cm) cakes

8 oz (225 g) unsalted softened butter

8 oz (225 g) caster sugar, sifted, plus extra for coating

4 fresh free-range eggs, weighing about 8 oz (225 g) when shelled

8 oz (225 g) self-raising flour, sifted, plus extra for dusting

Flavourings

finely grated rind of 1 orange plus 1 tablespoon juice

1 tablespoon Camp coffee essence

1 tablespoon cocoa powder

vanilla or almond essence (optional)

Filling

jam and/or whipped cream

Toppings

sifted icing sugar or flavoured icing or melted plain chocolate or buttercream (8 oz/225 g each of softened butter and icing sugar plus flavouring of your choice)

Pre-heat the oven to gas mark 4, 350 °F (180 °C).

Butter for baking should always be soft. By this I mean that when you push your thumb into it, the thumbprint clearly remains. Put the butter into a large mixing bowl and add the sugar. At this stage I think it best if you use your hands to combine these two ingredients. Do so until the mixture is light, fluffy and nearly white in colour when compared to its original yellow.

Break the eggs into a separate bowl and beat them gently (it is never a good idea to add eggs to a mix straight out of the shell). Add the beaten eggs to the mixture a little at a time while whisking, preferably with an electric hand whisk. Do this by dribbling just a little beaten egg over the creamed butter and sugar, and whisking until every single drop has vanished; stop the whisk, add a similar amount of egg and whisk again; repeat until all the egg is absorbed. This way you will get a creamy light texture.

The next stage, which needs infinite care, is the actual folding in of the sifted self-raising flour. I always say that you cannot cook well if you are in a bad mood – I firmly believe that cooking is a labour of love. Be tense and angry, and your cakes will turn out to be as heavy as lead. To fold in the flour I find I get much better results if I use a really long-handled spoon, which I hold at the very end of the handle – picture a fairy's wand! Take your time in gradually persuading the soft mix to incorporate all the flour.

When no sign of the flour remains, divide the mixture into four and place in separate bowls (photo 1), as you will be flavouring each portion differently. To the first add the grated orange rind plus 1 tablespoon fresh orange juice; to the second add 1 tablespoon coffee essence; to the third add 1 tablespoon cocoa powder (do not use drinking chocolate as the flavour won't come through); and to the fourth you can add a little vanilla or almond essence – but usually I don't add anything.

Lightly grease four 7 in (18 cm) sponge tins (I use the wrapping from the butter to do this) and coat on both base and sides with flour and caster sugar (photo 2).

1 Divide the sponge mixture into four.

2 Coat the greased tins with flour and sugar.

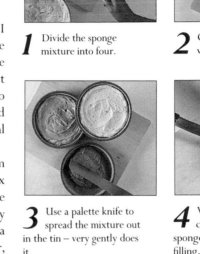

3 Use a palette knife to spread the mixture out in the tin – very gently does it.

4 When baked and cooled, split each sponge in half horizontally for filling, using a sharp bread knife.

Put the mixtures into the tins and spread evenly, *very gently*, with a palette knife (photo 3). Don't use any force or you will press the air out.

Bake in the pre-heated oven for 20–30 minutes. Gently open the oven door, remove one cake and test if it is cooked by putting the tip of a knife – or, better still, a skewer – into the centre. Whatever you use should be completely dry when removed if the sponge is cooked.

Leave the cakes in the tins for a few minutes to start cooling and then turn them out on to a cooling rack – you might need a palette knife to ease them. When cold, split each in two horizontally (photo 4). A bread knife is ideal for this, but go about it slowly and methodically, putting pressure on the knife only as you take it away from you.

Fill the sponges with jam or whipped cream, or both. Dust the tops with sifted icing sugar, ice with a flavoured icing, apply thin lines of melted chocolate or top with buttercream made by combining 8 oz (225 g) each of softened butter and icing sugar with a little flavouring to taste – coffee essence, booze, citrus rind and juice, etc.; sprinkle a few nuts over the buttercream.

Coffee cake

*T*HEY SAY NECESSITY is the mother of invention, and this is certainly the case as far as this recipe goes. I recently went over to the farm late one evening only to realise that some people were coming in for morning coffee and a nibble next day, and unfortunately the larder was bare of many basic essentials, including the liquid coffee essence that I always used when making cakes or other coffee-flavoured dishes. However, I was very agreeably surprised to find not only that freeze-dried instant coffee granules provide a delicious flavour, but also that the actual grittiness of the granules brings a new dimension to the texture of the end product.

Being low on butter the next morning, I was also fascinated to discover that Philadelphia cream cheese made a good substitute for the cream filling! You should be able to find this in the dairy section of any supermarket.

Makes 1 square 8 in (20 cm) or round 10 in (25 cm) cake

8 oz (225 g) caster sugar

8 oz (225 g) softened butter

4 heaped tablespoons freeze-dried instant coffee

4 or 6 eggs, lightly beaten (see method)

10 oz (275 g) self-raising flour, sifted

4 oz (100 g) ground hazelnuts

6 tablespoons dark rum (see method)

Cream filling

4 teaspoons freeze-dried instant coffee or 2 tablespoons Camp coffee essence

12 oz (350 g) Philadelphia cream cheese

4 oz (100 g) soft brown sugar

Pre-heat the oven to gas mark 4, 350°F (180°C), and line an 8 in (20 cm) square or 10 in (25 cm) round tin with a double thickness of greaseproof paper (photo 1).

Cream the sugar, butter and coffee together in a mixing bowl until light and fluffy (photo 2).

As for the eggs: if you would like a rum taste to the cake, use 4 eggs and fold the rum in at the end; if you're teetotal, or simply don't like the taste of rum, use 6 eggs. Add the beaten eggs to the mixture little by little, making absolutely sure, before you add any more, that what's gone in before has 'vanished'. If you charge through this part of the recipe like a bull in a china shop, woe betide you, as your mixture will invariably curdle. Don't panic and think of throwing it away: simply fold in some of the flour to stabilise it, then fold in a little more egg followed by flour until all are combined.

Fold in the sifted self-raising flour and ground hazelnuts using a long-handled spoon as described on p. 131 (photo 3), and if you used only 4 eggs and have opted for the rum, fold the latter in at the very end.

Pour the mixture into the prepared tin and, using a spatula, bring the mix away from the middle and slightly up the sides (photo 4). This way your cake will rise beautifully and *not* sink in the middle when cooling. Bake in the pre-heated oven for 45 minutes, then open the door carefully and test by inserting a metal meat skewer in the middle; if the cake is done, it should come out completely dry. If it doesn't, close the oven door with the utmost care without creating a draught and cook the cake for a little longer. When the cake is ready, remove and leave to cool.

To make the cream filling, dissolve the instant coffee granules (if using) in 1 tablespoon boiling water. (If using coffee essence, nothing need be added.) Cream together the cheese and sugar until very light and fluffy, add the coffee and mix thoroughly. Carefully split the cake horizontally into three rounds, using a sharp serrated knife and applying pressure as it goes into the cake, slicing away from you. (When the knife comes back towards you, it does not work.) Divide the coffee cream into two portions and use it to sandwich the cake circles together.

1 Line the tin – round or square – with a double thickness of greaseproof paper.

2 Cream the sugar, butter and coffee together until light and fluffy.

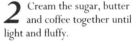

3 Mix in the eggs gradually, then carefully fold in the flour and hazelnuts with a long-handled spoon.

4 To ensure an even rising, draw the cake mixture in the tin slightly away from the centre and up the sides.

Shortbread

E*VERY HAPPY COOK and most cookery writers have their own version of shortbread, and all insist it is the best. Some people like shortbread cooked to a lightish shade of brown, and others say that it should come out of the oven the same colour as it went in.*

I give two recipes here, one for the fairly traditional tray of shortbread, to be cut into fingers, and one which can be made into little iced and jammed biscuits or tartlet cases to hold cream and soft fruit. If prepared in a food mixer, both take only minutes to make (provided the butter is very soft).

Makes about 1½ lb (700 g)

8 oz (225 g) plain flour, sifted, plus extra for dusting

4 oz (100 g) Farola or fine semolina

4 oz (100 g) caster sugar, plus extra for coating

8 oz (225 g) softened butter, plus extra for greasing

a little extra flour and sugar, and vanilla sugar (sugar stored and thus flavoured with a vanilla pod)

Pre-heat the oven to gas mark 3, 325°F (160°C). Have ready a Swiss roll tin approximately 8 × 11 in (20 × 28 cm), and ¾ in (2 cm) deep. If your tin is 10 × 12 in (25 × 30 cm), obviously the shortbread will be much thinner so will not need the full cooking time; likewise, if your tin is smaller, the shortbread will be thicker and the cooking time relatively longer.

Put the flour, Farola or semolina, sugar and butter into a food mixer (not a processor) and, using the biscuit beater on a slow speed, beat until you have a soft dough.

Lightly grease the Swiss roll tin and coat with plain flour. On top of this add a thin scattering of caster sugar. Take a small handful of the dough mix and press flat into the tin; repeat until all the mixture is used up. Put a sheet of good-quality greaseproof paper on top and, with a small rolling pin or jam jar, roll the mixture as flat as possible. Take the greaseproof paper off, and make firm thumbprints round the edge of the dough and then lots of impressions all over the central area with the end of a fork. Put in the fridge and leave to chill lightly.

Cook in the pre-heated oven for 1 hour. Remove the shortbread from the oven and, as it is cooling, sprinkle with vanilla sugar and cut into as many portions as you wish.

1 Use a 2½ in (6 cm) cutter to cut out both biscuits and tartlets.

2 Press rounds into appropriately sized tartlet tins.

3 Use a cup-cake paper containing uncooked rice (or something similar) as a weight for baking blind.

4 Remove paper and rice, and ease tartlets out of the tins before cooling, filling or lining with chocolate

Shortbread biscuits or tartlet cases

Makes 20–24 rounds

5 oz (150 g) plain flour

5 oz (150 g) self-raising flour, sifted, plus extra for dusting

3 oz (75 g) caster sugar

7 oz (200 g) softened butter

pinch of salt

For the biscuits

jam

icing

desiccated coconut, toasted

For the tartlets

plain chocolate, melted

fruit

whipped cream

Pre-heat the oven to gas mark 2, 300°F (150°C).

Place all the ingredients in a food mixer and, using the biscuit beater, slowly bring them together. Lightly flour the work surface and put half the mixture on to this. Gently roll out to a thickness of ¼ in (5 mm) and, using a 2½ in (6 cm) biscuit cutter, cut out the biscuits (photo 1).

Transfer to a baking tray and bake in the pre-heated oven for 30 minutes. Remove from the oven and transfer to a cooling tray. Serve as they are, or jam two together, put some icing on the top and scatter toasted desiccated coconut on them (see the main photo).

If you wish, you can use the other half of the mixture to make lovely tartlets. Roll and cut out as above and drop each circle of dough into a tartlet tin, pressing it down on to the base and up round the sides (photo 2). Then put a cup-cake paper containing uncooked rice (or anything similar) into the shortbread case to stop it from rising (photo 3). Bake as above.

Remove the paper and rice, gently ease the cooked tartlet cases out of the tin and leave to cool (photo 4). They *can* be stored as they are, but if you melt a little chocolate and paint the inside base and sides with it, they will be much stronger and less likely to break up. To serve, fill with fruit and whipped cream.

Home-made biscuits

*I*T IS A RELATIVELY SIMPLE task, for most people, to buy 'home-made' biscuits from their local delicatessen. Even easier, however, is spending 15 minutes yourself, and enjoying the complimentary comments as you see the plates emptying! Essential to all these three biscuits is very soft butter, and each recipe can be doubled up, allowing you to freeze or chill the balance. A good food mixer will do the job in a jiffy. If you haven't one, in each instance the fat should be rubbed into the flour and then you must use firm fist-force to knead the mixture to a dough.

Of course, your personal taste in ingredients can be followed once you have mastered the simple techniques. Orange rind, coffee powder, vanilla essence, ground hazelnuts or desiccated coconut could be added to both the fork and Viennoise biscuits, and the oatmeal ones could have dry English mustard or your own favourite spice included.

I haven't actually costed the recipes, but I am amazed at how many I seem to get for relatively little outlay, and home-made biscuits are infinitely superior to any mass-produced product.

Fork biscuits

These are served each day at Miller Howe on early-morning tea and coffee trays. I used to insist that the housekeepers put five biscuits on the plate for two guests, saying they could start the day as they wished to continue — by arguing over who should have the odd one!

Makes about 30

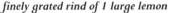

8 oz (225 g) softened butter

10 oz (275 g) self-raising flour, sifted

4 oz (100 g) caster sugar, plus extra for dusting

finely grated rind of 1 large lemon

1 For the fork biscuits, leave plenty of room on the baking tray to allow them to spread.

2 Using a dampened fork, press lightly into shape.

3 For the Viennoise biscuits, pipe into 3 in (7.5 cm) long strips – wiggly ones if you prefer!

4 After dipping in chocolate, hang the coated ends of the Viennoise biscuits over lip of a tray.

Pre-heat the oven to gas mark 4, 350°F (180°C), and line two baking trays with greaseproof paper.

Place all the ingredients in your mixing bowl and, with the beater on slow, mix to a softish dough. Break off *even-sized* balls and place these on the prepared tray, leaving plenty of space between each for them to spread (photo 1). Using the dampened base of a fork, lightly press them into shape (photo 2).

Bake in the pre-heated oven for 10 minutes. Remove the biscuits from the oven, place on a cooling rack and sprinkle with caster sugar as they cool. When cold, store in an air-tight container.

Biscuits for cheese

Makes about 22

6 oz (175 g) wheatmeal flour, plus extra for dusting

2 oz (50 g) coarse oats

2 oz (50 g) softened butter

2 oz (50 g) softened lard

2 heaped teaspoons caster sugar

1 heaped teaspoon baking powder

generous pinch of salt

1 heaped teaspoon curry powder

2 tablespoons cold milk

Pre-heat the oven to gas mark 4, 350°F (180°C), and line two baking trays with greaseproof paper.

Place all the ingredients in a food mixer and mix as for fork biscuits (see left). Flour a work surface and roll out the dough on it to approximately 12 × 10 in (30 × 25 cm). Using a 2 in (5 cm) round cutter, cut into circles. Bake in the pre-heated oven for 15 minutes, then leave to cool. Store in an air-tight tin.

Viennoise biscuits

Makes about 26

8 oz (225 g) softened butter

2 oz (50 g) icing sugar, sifted

8 oz (225 g) plain flour, sifted

4 oz (100 g) plain chocolate, melted with 1 tablespoon sherry or brandy

Pre-heat the oven to gas mark 4, 350°F (180°C), and line two baking trays with greaseproof paper.

Cream the soft butter with the icing sugar until light and fluffy, then, tablespoon by tablespoon, beat in the sifted flour.

Put the mixture into a piping bag with an eight-star nozzle and pipe out approximately 26 × 3 in (7.5 cm) long strips, leaving ample room for them to spread (photo 3).

Bake in the pre-heated oven for 15 minutes. Allow to cool, then dip the ends in the melted chocolate. Leave the coated ends hanging slightly over the lip of a tray (photo 4) until dry.

Miller Howe wholemeal bread

THIS VERY POPULAR bread is used for breakfast at the hotel, and once again is very easy to make (although it takes longer than the white variety). You will find this method very easy as there is no kneading involved. The texture is quite a lot denser than shop-bought wholemeal bread and much more delicious.

Makes 2 × 1 lb (450 g) loaves

1 lb (450 g) wholemeal flour

2 teaspoons salt

2 tablespoons black treacle

10 fl oz (300 ml) plus 2 tablespoons warm water

1 oz (25 g) fresh yeast

oil for greasing

Sift the wholemeal flour and salt into a large bowl. In another smaller bowl mix the treacle with the 2 tablespoons warm water and sprinkle the fresh yeast on top. Put somewhere warm and out of draughts for 10 minutes, after which it should have developed a head like that on a good glass of Guinness. Simply add the remaining warm water to this, pouring it all over the flour. Using a long-handled spoon, combine to a dough, then divide between two greased 1 lb (450 g) loaf tins. Cover with greaseproof paper and leave again somewhere warm for about 30 minutes until the dough virtually doubles in size.

Meanwhile pre-heat the oven to gas mark 6, 400°F (200°C). Bake in the oven for approximately 40 minutes. Leave on a cooling tray until cold.

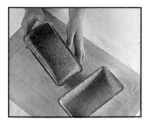

1 You can sprinkle extra sesame seeds on to the greased base and sides of the tins if you like.

2 Add the dry ingredients to the food mixer bowl, mixing very slowly.

3 Divide the mix between the two seeded loaf tins.

Brown yoghurt seed loaf

M Y MAIN MEMORIES of childhood are connected with food, and most of all I vividly remember an enormous, well-used pot bowl which seemed always to be in the hearth by the open fire and oven, with bread dough of some kind or other rising in it. The smell of newly baked loaves, baps, tea-cakes, currant cobs and malt slices pervades my nostrils even now!

So many people seem to think bread-making is difficult, time-consuming and tiresome. Nothing could be further from the truth, particularly if you like the taste and texture of Irish soda bread which traditionally uses buttermilk and bicarbonate of soda as the raising agent. But when I found myself recently at the farm without yeast in any shape or form (I normally have small 2 oz/50 g lumps of fresh yeast in the freezer), I had to come up with the following recipe. It should appeal to lazy cooks, and to those intent on wholesome, 'nutty' food. The beauty of the recipe is that, once you have tried it, it can be easily adapted to personal taste: if it is too sweet, for instance,

use less treacle and more olive oil. I once used honey when I was out of treacle. I have used chopped walnuts and hazelnuts at times, and if I have any raisins or sultanas soaking in brandy, they certainly enhance the end product! You can also vary the seed content; and if using sunflower seeds, these benefit from a 15-minute toasting in a medium oven. It is, however, important to leave the bread to go quite cold before attempting to slice it.

Makes 2 × 1 lb (450 g) loaves

2 oz (50 g) self-raising flour
7 oz (200 g) wheatmeal flour
1 teaspoon bicarbonate of soda
½ teaspoon salt
4 heaped tablespoons in all of sunflower, sesame and poppy seeds, plus extra sesame seeds for coating
1 egg, lightly beaten
7½ fl oz (225 ml) natural yoghurt
3 tablespoons black treacle
2 teaspoons olive oil, plus extra for greasing

Pre-heat the oven to gas mark 5, 375°F (190°C), and grease two 1 lb (450 g) loaf tins with oil. You can, if you like, scatter extra sesame seeds into the tins, allowing them to cover both base and sides (photo 1).

Sift together the flours, bicarbonate of soda and salt in a mixing bowl, add the 4 tablespoons seeds and mix well. Combine the remaining ingredients in the bowl of a food mixer and add the dry ingredients to this while the mixer is on the slowest speed possible (photo 2). You'll be amazed at how soon the mixture comes together.

Place the prepared tins on a thin baking tray and divide the combined mix (it does bubble a little!) equally between them (photo 3).

Bake in the pre-heated oven for 45 minutes. Remove from the oven, having tested first with the sharp end of a knife to check that the mixture is completely dry: the knife should come out clean. About 10 minutes after they have come out of the oven, turn the loaves out of their tins on to a cooling rack, but do not attempt to cut them until they are stone cold.

Cream sauces

*I*N THIS RECIPE *I might well be tempting born-again health-food addicts to rush for their recycled notepaper and write furious letters.*

I hold up my hands and admit defeat now — yes, 1 pint (600 ml) double cream for six to eight people is terribly extravagant. And as for three-quarters of a bottle of white wine — hell's bells and buckets of blood! But this is intended for that special occasion when you really want to impress.

This sauce can safely be made an hour ahead of time provided it is kept in a warm, secure place — in the warming drawer of your stove, covered in the boiler room, or even in a hot airing cupboard — but it most not on any account be allowed to cool down before serving: it will simply set and can then be revived only with extreme difficulty.

If you follow my advice, however, the sauce will behave itself and be the highlight of your dinner party; it should never split, curdle or go lumpy. It is rich, I admit, so consider carefully the courses to be served on either side.

Serves 6–8

1 pint (600 ml) double cream

pinch of salt

flavouring (see opposite)

Put the cream and salt into a fairly large saucepan (photo 1). Normally when using a saucepan, of course, you would place it completely over the hot hob. In this case, however, you must place only about a third of the pan over direct heat (photo 2), because when the cream reaches the vital temperature, it has the unruly habit of coming suddenly to the boil and surging over the edge of the pan like the head on a badly served bottle of Guinness.

Watch it like a hawk and, depending on the heat of the hob, your cream will be reduced by half in 15–20 minutes (photo 3). Do not take it any further and lo and behold, your basic sauce is made! Now to complete the sauce, add one of the flavourings suggested on the opposite page.

FLAVOURINGS

1 Pour the cream and salt into a fairly large saucepan.

2 Only a third of the saucepan should be over direct heat, as cream boils over so easily.

3 Reduce the cream like this, stirring every now and then, until reduced by half.

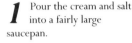

4 For a classic sauce, mix in the reduced wine flavouring as described.

For an inexpensive but tangy flavour simply beat in 2 tablespoons tomato purée and 1 tablespoon dry English mustard. This is the sauce that I've used in the main picture to cover my vegetable casserole (see p. 98).

For a truly classic white wine sauce, however, this is what you must do. Earlier in the day you will have set aside three-quarters of a bottle of your chosen wine. I have occasionally seen people turn up their noses at a cheap wine, saying, 'It'll do for cooking.' But if they don't wish to upset their stomachs by drinking it, why should they think it won't offend them if they cook with it?

I don't for a moment suggest that you should cook with a great bottle of white burgundy, but do use a favourite, not a reject. Add 6 black peppercorns and simmer uncovered until the wine is reduced to just less than 5 fl oz (150 ml). The taste when it is mixed into the cream (photo 4) will be strong. Should you wish to flavour the cream with sherry, Marsala or Madeira instead of wine, start with just half a bottle, reducing this to a little under 5 fl oz (150 ml).

The completed sauce will hold in a bowl over simmering water for up to an hour, but keep checking it and giving it a good stir with an electric hand whisk.

This sauce is absolutely marvellous with breast of chicken, pork chops and many fish dishes. If you use Noilly Prat as the flavouring and add some finely chopped chives, it is admirable with baked salmon steaks.

Home-made mayonnaise

AT THE HOTEL I always insist on scrupulous kitchen hygiene, and as a result of following health inspectors' guidelines, the kitchen now resembles a clinical operating room rather than simply a clean operational area. I will agree to any sensible measures to avoid the dreaded salmonella, but I would throw in the towel if I were prevented from making custards, cream ices, hollandaise sauce, trifles, mousses, soufflés . . . and mayonnaise.

Nothing compares to home-made mayonnaise: it is infinitely superior to bottled, as well as being cheaper. It is thick, colourful and glowing, and it talks to you as you spoon it out of the serving dish – a satisfying noise like that of wet wellies being dragged off tired wet feet!

The first thing you must decide is what type of oil suits your pocket and palate – olive, groundnut, grapeseed or whatever. The next thing is to find a reliable source of really fresh, free-range farm eggs. In the Lakes there are plenty of outlets, as there are in the Rossendale Valley where I have my farmhouse. When Bobby Lyons was head chef at Miller Howe, he used to bring in eggs laid the day before on his smallholding to be cooked for breakfast. The rich orange colour of the yolks actually put some folk off, but oh, the taste!

Makes 10 fl oz (300 ml)

2 large fresh egg yolks

1 level teaspoon soft free-running salt

1 level teaspoon dry English mustard

1 level teaspoon caster sugar

2 teaspoons fresh lemon juice

10 fl oz (300 ml) oil of your choice

white wine vinegar up to about 1 tablespoon

Place the egg yolks, salt, mustard, sugar and lemon juice in a small bowl and set the bowl on a damp cloth to prevent it slithering about (photo 1). Have the oil ready in a measuring jug.

Start beating the mixture with an electric beater and dip your other hand into the oil. Let the oil dribble very slowly into the bowl from the tips of your fingers (photo 2). Do this very, very slowly, because if you rush the operation, your mayonnaise will curdle. Should such a disaster occur, don't, whatever you do, throw it away – it can be saved. Simply tip the mess out into another bowl, clean the original bowl, and start with another egg yolk. Beat into this, little by little, the curdled mix.

1 Put the egg yolks, salt, mustard, sugar and lemon juice in a bowl and set the bowl on a damp cloth to prevent it slithering about.

2 Using an electric hand beater, start dribbling the oil into the bowl – with your fingers!

3 When about two-thirds of the oil has been incorporated, the mayonnaise will be rather thick and stodgy.

4 Store the mayonnaise in a screw-top jar in the fridge for up to a week.

Dribble the oil in very slowly, and when you have incorporated about two-thirds of it into the mix – which should now be thick and stodgy (photo 3) – add a teaspoon of the wine vinegar. Add the balance of the oil – rather more swiftly than before – with the beater on full speed. When it is all in, taste the mayonnaise, and if you think it needs more vinegar, add some. If you pour the mayonnaise into a screw-top jar (photo 4), it will keep safely in the fridge for up to a week.

For greater speed you can use a food processor to make the mayonnaise if you must. Instead of egg yolks, use whole eggs, and trickle in the oil at a steady pace. The texture is never the same – nor is the job satisfaction.

VARIATIONS

You can alter the flavouring of your mayonnaise. You could use more or less mustard or sugar; or a different vinegar such as garlic, mint or tarragon. You could incorporate 2 tablespoons finely chopped fresh herbs, or 1 tablespoon tomato purée; the mashed flesh of a very ripe avocado makes a delicious and subtle avocado mayonnaise; or you could add the finely grated rind and juice of a lemon or an orange – always experiment!

French dressings

*F*RENCH READERS *are likely to take the book back to the shop and ask for their money back when they realise that the only French thing about my French dressing is the name — which derives from America!*

French dressings should be fun. I never have the same dressing twice in succession, and there's always a couple of jars of it in my cupboard. When the volume gets low, I pour them back into the liquidiser and start 'playing' again.

I am frequently asked how long a dressing will keep, and the answer is 'as long as the ingredients'. Using just the basic ingredients, however, the liquid will last for ages. It is only when you introduce fresh herbs and rich oils that the keeping time is reduced.

Dressings can be served hot or cold. Weight-conscious folk can thin them with rosé wine — but not enough to dilute the distinctive flavour.

For the most basic French dressing you require only wine vinegar, olive oil, salt, pepper, dry English mustard and a little sugar. Your favoured oil will be one that suits both your palate and your pocket: apart from olive it could be sesame, grapeseed, corn, walnut, hazelnut, avocado, macadamia . . . even bacon fat or the fat saved from roasting the duck on p. 92. The vinegar should always be a wine one, never malt, and it's commonly said that for the basic recipe the ratio of oil to vinegar should be four to one. This is too sharp for me, so I use a little less vinegar. If you opt for the usual ratio, though, and want to make only a very small amount of dressing, use 1 scant tablespoon of vinegar to 4 tablespoons oil and just a pinch of the other ingredients. Shake well together in a screw-top jar.

Now comes the time when you will be tasting overtime to check how the concoction develops. Don't be inhibited. If there's something in the larder you

particularly like, add it to the mix: honey, home-made stock, fresh herbs, garlic purée, hard-boiled eggs, watercress, sorrel. You'll see a few of the additional ingredients in the main picture. Just remember that these will diminish the shelf-life of the end product. So the golden rule is – experiment!

However, I always make over 1½ pints (900 ml) at a time in the liquidiser, using 4 tablespoons wine vinegar, 1 pint (600 ml) of the chosen oil, 1 level teaspoon each of caster sugar, dry English mustard and free-running salt, and a generous pinch of cayenne pepper. Whizz everything around and adjust the basic seasoning as necessary.

Now is the time to be bold with additions to the basic mix. The flavour changes dramatically, for example, if you add 5 fl oz (150 ml) walnut or hazelnut oil. A couple of tablespoons of your favourite runny honey will give a touch of sweetness. A tablespoon of raspberry vinegar added last will transform the dressing again – and so on. Don't forget all the aforementioned ingredients, or any others that occur to you.

SKINNING TOMATOES

For the salads that your wonderful French dressings will accompany, skinned tomatoes are a must. Whether you slice, quarter or chop them, the preparation is easy, as shown in the step-by-step photos.

Have ready a small saucepan of boiling water and make a criss-cross cut in the skin at the base of each tomato (photo 1). Very firm tomatoes should also have a little of the stalk end removed. Submerge in the boiling water for 4–5 seconds (a little longer for very firm tomatoes) and then transfer to a bowl of cold water (photo 2). It is then relatively easy to remove the skin using a small, sharp knife (photo 3). Cut in half and under the cold tap, push out the seeds (photo 4), using a teaspoon if you like.

1 Make a criss-cross cut in the skin of the tomato and dunk into boiling water for 4–5 seconds.

2 Transfer to a bowl of cold water.

3 Peel back the skin from the criss-cross cut.

4 Push out the seeds from the halved tomatoes under cold running water (you could use a teaspoon).

Curry essence

*P*ACKETS OF CURRY *powder are readily available and, provided they are used very quickly after opening, can produce the desired effect. However, a real Indian curry is concocted by bringing together some of the following basic ingredients in either powdered or crushed form, or as an essence.*

ALLSPICE:

The dried berry of the allspice tree, a member of the pepper family, sometimes called Jamaica pepper.

ANISEED:

A pungent seed and a member of the parsley family.

BAY LEAF:

The aromatic leaves of the sweet bay or bay laurel.

CAPSICUMS:

There are nearly 200 varieties of these peppers, ranging from sweet to chilli (see below).

CARDAMOM:

The seed-containing pods of a large perennial herb which belongs to the ginger family.

CHILLI:

The fresh or dried fruit of many varieties of capsicum, one of the hottest flavourings known.

CINNAMON:

The inner bark of a small tropical evergreen tree.

CLOVES:

The dried flowerbuds of an evergreen tree, a member of the myrtle family.

CORIANDER:

An attractive herbal plant, whose seeds provide the flavouring. (The leaves are useful too.)

CUMIN:

The pungent seeds of a delicate herb, which look rather similar to caraway.

GARLIC:

A pungent bulbous member of the onion family.

GINGER:

The rhizomes or root of a lily-like tropical plant, available fresh, dried, crystallised and powdered.

MACE:

The husk of the nutmeg.

MUSTARD SEED:

As the name suggests.

NUTMEG:

The seed of the nutmeg tree, which also produces mace.

PEPPERCORNS:

The fruit of a tropical vine. Black and white come from the same berry, black from the dried unripe fruit, white from the ripe.

SAFFRON:

Some 24,000 crocus stigmas will give you just 1 lb (450 g) saffron – hence its price and its rarity.

TURMERIC:

The rhizomes of a plant of the ginger family, used mainly for colouring.

The joy I get from making curry essence is in changing it slightly every time and thus achieving a different taste. This basic recipe will allow just that – it can be added to and subtracted from. The secret is to experiment.

The essence can be stored in a screw-top jar and added to your curries, to double-cream reductions for cream sauces, to hollandaise and mayonnaise.

2 tablespoons olive oil
2 oz (50 g) butter
4 oz (100 g) onions, peeled and finely chopped
1/4 teaspoon ground allspice
2 bay leaves
3 cardamom pods (seeds only)
2 × 1 in (2.5 cm) cinnamon sticks
4 cloves
1 tablespoon coriander seeds
1 teaspoon chilli powder
2 garlic cloves, crushed with 1 teaspoon free-running salt
1 teaspoon mustard seeds
6 black peppercorns
1 teaspoon ground turmeric
5 fl oz (150 ml) red wine
2 tablespoons apricot jam

Heat the oil and butter in a pan and fry the onions until golden. Add all the remaining ingredients except for the wine and jam and cook over a high heat for several minutes (photo 1). Stir well, add the wine and jam, and then simmer for 5 minutes. Liquidise and pass through a coarse sieve (photo 2).

The essence can now be used in the quantity that you decide will achieve the desired flavour. For instance, I like to make a curry mayonnaise (see p. 166 for the basic mayonnaise recipe): simply stir in some of the curry essence (photo 3). To make this even lighter, the mix can be 'let down' with lightly whipped double cream (photo 4).

1 Most of the ingredients are cooked together over a high heat to release their flavours.

2 When the cooking is finished, liquidise the essence and pass through a coarse sieve into a bowl or jar.

3 To pep up a mayonnaise, simply stir in curry essence to taste.

4 To make a curry mayonnaise lighter, simply fold in some lightly whipped double cream.

Decadent hot milk

I CAN THINK of no better way to end a winter's day than to have an early night in bed with a good book, using the remote control to flick the telly from channel to channel, and having a very boozy and comforting milk drink. The older I get, the more of these self-indulgences I allow myself as I am then able to cope better the next day with all my various trials and tribulations! The hot milk is also super to take in vacuum flasks when going on long winter walks.

A liquidiser makes all the difference to the milk nightcap, its whizzing blades creating more volume and a frothy topping. Hot milk reminds me of wartime shopping trips to Barrow-in-Furness as they ended with a visit to Brucciani's Italian ice-cream parlour. This was where Barrow café society dillied and dallied, where daily news of which shop had what in at what price was exchanged, and who was doing what with whom! A huge, highly polished, copper steamer hissed noisily as the endless Horlicks and Ovaltine beakers were placed under the nozzles which heated the drinks and added the froth.

Per decadent person

2 tablespoons brandy or rum

2 teaspoons soft brown sugar

2 tablespoons double cream (optional)

2 level teaspoons cocoa powder (not drinking chocolate)

cold milk

freshly ground nutmeg

finely grated rind of 1 orange

½ oz (15 g) good-quality plain chocolate, grated

Place the spirit, sugar, cream and cocoa powder in a large beaker and top up near to the rim with cold milk. Transfer to a liquidiser and whizz at high speed. Pour into a saucepan and bring to the boil over a medium heat. Return to the liquidiser, add a generous sprinkling of grated nutmeg and the orange rind, and whizz again. Pour the mixture back into the beaker and garnish with grated chocolate.

Hot toddy

At the very first sign of a sniffle in the cold months, I reach for a hot toddy. Personally I always use a lovely cut-glass crystal tumbler and finest malt whisky, but blended Scotch, brandy or rum can be substituted. Those of you who have signed the pledge must, obviously, avoid the booze; substitute 3 well-crushed cloves, lots of freshly grated nutmeg and a small cinnamon stick. If you don't have a sweet tooth, omit the sugar, but do use the honey.

Per poorly person

1 generous measure of malt whisky

juice of ¹/₂ lemon

¹/₂ teaspoon soft brown sugar

1 teaspoon free-running honey

Warm a glass and mix together in it the whisky, lemon juice, sugar and honey. Top up with boiling water – you need about three times the volume of the whisky.

Spiced fruit cup

*T*HIS IS A DELICIOUS *fruity hot drink which is ideal for a winter party or barbecue. Serve it in 10 fl oz (300 ml) beer mugs. Guests should use their fingers to dig out the fruits once they've drunk the wine!*

Serves 12

12 dried apricots

5 fl oz (150 ml) cooking brandy

2 bottles light red wine

1 lb (450 g) caster sugar

the peel of 1 lemon and 1 orange, cut off in strips with a scorer

1 whole nutmeg, finely grated

6 cloves

2 cinnamon sticks, broken into 2 in (5 cm) pieces

Calvados and apple juice punch

Cheap Calvados can be rough on its own, but here's a delicious out-of-the-ordinary punch using it. For each measure of Calvados, use five of apple juice. Place the Calvados in a punch bowl or glass dish and scatter in thin slices of cored dessert apples. Pour on the hot apple juice. A little pinch of powdered sage adds an unusual flavour.

Garnishes

melon balls, pear slices, apple slices, orange wedges, seeded grapes.

Soak the apricots overnight in the brandy.

Pour the wine into a large saucepan and add the sugar along with the strips of lemon and orange peel, nutmeg, cloves and cinnamon. Simmer for 10 minutes.

Warm the mugs and generously garnish with the assorted fruits, including the plumped-up apricots. Pass the hot wine through a fine plastic sieve into a jug then pour into the warmed, fruit-filled mugs.

Orange marmalade

A T THE MARMALADE time of year — end of January, beginning of February — the main kitchen at Miller Howe is like a witches' coven as four large cauldron-like pans are on the go every single day of the week in order to make the 1,200 lb (540 kg) of marmalade we seem to get through each season. The whole house smells like an orangery — and a good thing too as it helps to get rid of the paint smell that also pervades the place at this time: each January every single room, every nook and cranny, is painstakingly painted by the staff. This vast amount of marmalade is stored in huge plastic containers up in the attic, and keeps guests happy throughout the season.

I sometimes add marmalade to the apples in a farmhouse apple pie (see p. 148), and use it to make a hot sweet sauce to go with a steamed sponge pudding (8 oz/225 g marmalade brought to a simmer with 5 fl oz/150 ml dry white wine). However, nothing beats home-made marmalade when it is spread on lavishly buttered, piping-hot toast or Lakeland baps straight from the oven!

Here are a few points to remember when making marmalade.

1. If the citrus fruits are chilled, they will not produce quite so much juice, so keep them at room temperature.

2. It is the fruit's pectin that sets the preserve, and so you should use every piece of pulp and pith, and every pip.

3. A long simmering is best to tenderise the strips of peel.

4. Add the sugar 1 lb (450 g) at a time away from the heat, and don't add more until it is all dissolved, otherwise the marmalade will go sugary while it is being stored.

5. Once all the sugar has dissolved, return the pan to a very high heat.

6. Leave the finished marmalade to cool slightly before potting.

The following quantities will make about 10 lb (4.5 kg) of marmalade. You can, actually, use up to 12 lb (5.5 kg) sugar if you like, which results in a much sweeter and lighter-coloured marmalade — as well as more.

Makes about 10 lb (4.5 kg)

6 lb (2.75 kg) fresh Seville oranges at room temperature

2 lemons at room temperature

6 pints (3.5 litres) cold water

6 lb (2.75 kg) preserving sugar

Have ready ten to twelve spotlessly clean and warm 1 lb (450 g) jam jars, and the same number of waxed paper circles, cellophane circles and rubber bands.

Wipe the oranges and lemons thoroughly with a damp cloth and dry well. Cut all the fruit in half horizontally (photo 1): do not cut through the stalk as it will then be difficult to remove all the flesh. Squeeze out as much juice as possible and put it in a large plastic mixing bowl. Spread a clean teatowel on the work surface and, using a tablespoon (preferably silver), scrape out all the pith and pips on to it, leaving just skin and scraps of flesh. Bring the four corners of the teatowel together and tie them.

Cut the orange and lemon skin halves in half again. Cut the quarters into very thin strips and add these to the juice in the bowl. Place the teatowel 'ball' into the middle of the juice/peel mixture, cover with a cloth or tinfoil and leave somewhere cold overnight.

You now require a large saucepan (preferably stainless steel) and this must be perfectly clean: rub with a half-lemon sprinkled with a little salt to ensure that it is free of grease. Into this place the orange and lemon juice and rind, the water and the teatowel bag – the last of these suspended on a length of bamboo or wood laid across the top of the pan (photo 2). Using a felt-tip pen, mark the level of the pan's contents on its outside, because you must now bring them to the boil and simmer until reduced by half – probably for at least 2 hours.

When you have reduced the pan's contents, take it off the heat, press the bag tightly against the side of the pan to squeeze out the pectin and discard the bag. Beat in the preserving sugar (do not use any other kind) as described in point 4 above (photo 3).

Return the pan to the heat, bring to the boil and boil rapidly for 15–20 minutes. Have to hand a couple of very cold saucers. Put a tablespoon of the mix on to one, leave for a few minutes and then push it with your finger – it should be set; the surface should crinkle slightly as you push it and stay that way. If it doesn't, try again with the other saucer, perhaps repeating the test a third time until you get the desired effect (photo 4). (Keep the marmalade boiling meanwhile.) Now the marmalade is almost ready for potting. Remove it from the heat to cool slightly.

Filling the warm jam jars used to be a very messy job, but I was inundated with tips about special metal jam pourers. (In this business, you're always learning!). Fill the jars to the rim and, while still warm, cover with waxed paper circles. Moisten one side of each cellophane circle and put one firmly over the rim of each jar, moist side down, fixing it in place with a rubber band.

Store the jars in a cool place, and enjoy the fruits of your labours throughout the year!

1 Cut the fruits in half through their 'equators'.

2 Suspend the bag of pith and pips from a stick laid across the top of the pan.

3 Beat in the preserving sugar, 1 lb (450 g) at a time, *off the heat*.

4 To test for setting, place a little of the mix on a cold saucer. If it wrinkles, it's ready.

Snacks and canapés

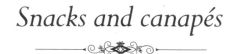

S*NACKS AND CANAPÉS are fiddly and can be time-consuming to make, I admit, but I find them well worth the effort. Most of the preparation can be done ahead of time, leaving just the simple, pleasant task of assembling them.*

If you feel so inclined, it takes very little time to bake individual pastry tartlet cases (use the savoury pastry on p. 146), but an even easier way is to make cases from very thin, well-buttered and flavoured slices of bread — a tip I discovered at a friend's birthday party.

You can use fairy-cake tins or smaller ones. For 24 canapés use 12 thin slices bread and 3 oz (75 g) melted butter flavoured with ½ teaspoon mustard and 1 teaspoon lemon juice. Cut the crusts off the bread and, using your heaviest rolling pin, flatten each slice and spread it as thin as it will go. To cut the bread into circles, use a round cutter slightly larger than the top diameter of your containers (I use a 2½ in/6 cm cutter and 1¾ in/4.5 cm tins). Dip each round of bread into the melted, flavoured butter and then mould firmly into the tins. Cook for 30 minutes in an oven pre-heated to gas mark 4, 350°F (180°C). When cool, the cases can be stored in an airtight container for up to a week.

I have simply piped duck pâté into mine and garnished them with a slice of stuffed olive. The little pastry tartlets contain piped Philadelphia cheese mixed with a small amount of horseradish cream and topped with Keta. If this is unobtainable, lumpfish roe will do nicely; garnish with sprigs of parsley.

The mini Swiss rolls and smoked salmon triangles are made from 2 lb (900 g) loaves. Chill them in the fridge and slice them lengthways. To do this, saw through the loaf with a sharp serrated knife, making each cut ¼ in (5 mm) above the work surface and using force only as you thrust the knife *away* from you. Remove the crusts and flatten the slices with a heavy rolling pin. Spread with butter and add the filling, such as cheese and herb pâté (see p. 16). Roll up the bread along the longer side to make cigar shapes. These can be wrapped in cling film or tinfoil, chilled and then sliced into circles.

For the open smoked salmon triangles, prepare brown bread in the same way (a little lemon juice added to the butter is nice), cover each long slice with smoked salmon and press this firmly on the bread. Divide each slice in two lengthways and then into triangles. Garnish with lemon slices and dill or fennel leaves.

Savoury cheese cubes

*T*HESE CAN BE *prepared ahead of time but baked at the last moment.*

3 oz (75 g) soft, full-fat cream cheese

4 oz (100 g) Cheddar cheese, coarsely grated

8 oz (225 g) softened butter

1 × 2 lb (1 kg) white loaf

2 egg whites

Melt the cheeses and butter together in a double saucepan. Remove the crusts from the loaf and discard; cut the bread into 1 in (2.5 cm) cubes. Beat the egg whites in a bowl until stiff and gently fold into the soft mixture. Using a cocktail stick, dip the bread cubes in this and place them on a baking tray. At this stage they can be gently covered with cling film and left in the fridge until needed.

Pre-heat the oven to gas mark 5, 375°F (190°C). Bake the cubes in the pre-heated oven for 15–20 minutes and serve while still warm.

Sesame cheese sables

12 oz (350 g) softened butter

12 oz (350 g) wheatmeal flour

12 oz (350 g) tasty hard cheese, finely grated

1 rounded teaspoon dry English mustard

¼ teaspoon salt

2 generous pinches of grated nutmeg

6 grindings of black pepper

sesame seeds and beaten egg

Pre-heat the oven to gas mark 4, 350°F (180°C).

Rub the butter into the flour and combine with the other ingredients – except the sesame and beaten egg – to make a dough. Divide the dough into two balls and chill.

Bring back to room temperature and roll out to ⅛ in (3 mm) thickness. The children can help by cutting out seasonal shapes – like our Christmas trees in the photo. Lightly brush these shapes with egg and then sprinkle with sesame seeds. Transfer to baking trays and bake in the pre-heated oven for 15–20 minutes.

Roast turkey

*Y*EARS AGO I COOKED *this on one of the late Russell Harty's Christmas at Home television programmes. The whole day spent recording the programme was great fun – even though it was November! All the stars kept coming over to the kitchen, as the smells were making their nostrils twitch – or it could have been because of the brandy and sherry I had hidden under the sink! The late Arthur Marshall was hilariously funny, the Great Soprendo had us in stitches with his tricks, and Edna O'Brien tried to keep us all in order.*

That year I also recorded five Cooking for Christmas *programmes for Radio 4's* Woman's Hour. *I missed the first two broadcasts but on the Wednesday tuned in just as Sue MacGregor was starting to tell us of listeners' comments: 'Is the man mad, using all that cream and butter?'; 'How can you have such extravagant dishes when people in the world are starving?'; 'Everything seems to centre around booze.' Sue introduced my third contribution in her inimitable, cool way: 'Oh dear, listeners, John is going to tell you today how to cook your turkey using 1½ lb butter!' For some reason·I have never been asked back on the programme.*

The joy of this recipe is that the bird is prepared at least the day before and you simply have to pop it in the oven 4½ hours before you intend to eat it.

Serves up to 12

1 oven-ready fresh turkey, weighing 12–14 lb (5.5–6.5 kg)

2 large carrots

1 large onion

1 apple

1½ lb (700 g) softened salted butter

1 small bunch of parsley

2 teaspoons salt

freshly ground black pepper

You will need a double thickness of butter muslin (haberdashery departments sell it), 30 in (75 cm) square. After the Harty programme, John Lewis in Oxford Street sold out in 4 days!

Lay both pieces of muslin on top of each other on the work surface and place the turkey, breast upwards, in the middle. Peel the carrots and skin the onion (remembering that clean peelings can be used in your stockpot) and cut it in half. Wipe and quarter the apple. Place all these inside the bird along with 8 oz (225 g) of the soft butter (photo 1) and the parsley.

Smear the remaining butter all over the skin of the turkey, remembering to get right down between the thighs, sprinkle with salt and be very generous with pepper (photo 2).

Draw one corner of the muslin up over the turkey breast and secure it with a wooden cocktail stick (photo 3). Then do the opposite corner, followed by the remaining two corners until the bird is covered (photo 4). You can do this quite far in advance; keep in a cool, safe place.

Pre-heat the oven to gas mark 4, 350°F (180°C). Place the turkey, breast upwards, in a roasting tin – you want the muslin to soak up all the fat and juices so that the bird self-bastes – and cook for 4 hours. Open the oven after an hour to baste the muslin.

At the end of the cooking time this does look pretty tacky (photo 5), but when you carefully remove the muslin, the end result is beautiful. Leave the turkey to rest for 30 minutes in the warm kitchen before you carve.

Apricot stuffing

You can include 6 oz (175 g) finely chopped chicken liver to make this even richer.

8 oz (225 g) onions, peeled and finely chopped

4 oz (100 g) smoked bacon, finely chopped

4 oz (100 g) butter

4 oz (100 g) dried apricots, soaked overnight in 2 tablespoons brandy (optional) and coarsely chopped

12 oz (350 g) sausagemeat

2 oz (50 g) breadcrumbs

Fry the onions and bacon in the butter until softened. Stir in the apricots and sausagemeat and simmer for 15 minutes. Combine with the breadcrumbs and, when cold, transfer to a suitable dish as above. Chill until ready to cook (see following recipe).

1 Place the turkey on doubled muslin, then put the carrots, halved onion, quartered apple and a third of the butter inside it.

2 Smear the remaining soft butter all over the bird and season well with salt and pepper.

3 Draw one corner of the muslin over the breast of the bird and secure in place using a wooden cocktail stick.

4 Do the same with the opposite corner, then the other two corners, to enclose the bird completely.

5 Beneath the messy muslin, after 4 hours, is a perfectly cooked turkey.

Apple, orange and watercress stuffing

*B*OTH THIS *and the previous stuffing need to be re-heated for 20–30 minutes in an oven pre-heated to gas mark 4, 350°F (180°C).*

---

6 oz (175 g) onions, peeled and finely chopped

---

4 oz (100 g) butter

---

1 lb (450 g) apples, peeled, cored and thinly sliced

---

finely grated rind of 2 oranges

---

juice of 1 orange

---

1 bunch of watercress, coarsely chopped

---

3 oz (75 g) breadcrumbs

Fry the onions in the butter until softened. Add the apples and orange rind and juice, and simmer for 30 minutes. Fold in the watercress and breadcrumbs. When cold, transfer to a suitable dish that can be used for re-heating as above, and store in a cold place until ready to cook.

Port, wine and cranberry sauce

1 lb (450 g) whole cranberries (fresh or frozen)
15 fl oz (450ml) red wine
5 fl oz (150 ml) port
1 oz (25 g) caster sugar
finely grated rind of 2 oranges
juice of 1 orange
4 teaspoons arrowroot mixed with 6 tablespoons cold water

If using frozen cranberries, spread them out on a tray and bring to room temperature, but do not let them get soggy.

Put the wine, port, sugar, orange rind and juice into a saucepan and dissolve the sugar over heat. Bring the wine mixture to the boil and add the arrowroot-and-water paste. Stir quite swiftly with a wooden spoon until thickened. Carefully fold in the cranberries and warm through.

Gravies

*G*RAVIES CAN BE GRIM *when you are entertaining – all that business of taking the roast out of the oven and allowing it to rest, draining off most of the fat, putting the roasting tin on the hob, adding your flour and vigorously incorporating all the sticky, crusty bits round the edge of the roasting tin, then adding your liquid and stirring frantically to prevent any lumps from forming.*

This does, I admit, make splendid gravy, but if you follow my recipe you can make quite a lot ahead of time and simply store it sensibly. If it is going to be used within a few days, put it in a screw-top jar in the fridge; if you need to keep it longer, put it in a marked container in the freezer.

Obviously you aren't going to have turkey before Christmas, so you can use a chicken carcass for the stock for this gravy. Make it as described on p. 10 – adding a bay leaf, a coarsely chopped clove of garlic and a handful of parsley as well – but collect beforehand double the quantities of the vegetable peelings and flavourings. You want some for the stock itself and about 1 lb (450 g) for the gravy. The aim is to finish up with 2–3 pints (1.2–1.75 litres) strained chicken stock for the gravy.

Likewise, whenever you are to have a weekend joint, follow this method and you will never again have the hassle of last-minute gravy making. If you seek a thin gravy, use 3 pints (1.75 litres) stock; if, like me, you prefer your gravy to have lots of body, use only 2 pints (1.2 litres).

---

4 oz (100 g) butter

1 lb (450 g) clean vegetable peelings

4 oz (100 g) plain flour, sifted

2–3 pts (1.2–1.75 litres) stock

In a thick-based saucepan melt the butter and add the peelings. Cook over a medium heat until they are well browned. Add the flour and once again cook – stirring from time to time – until the flour is brown and integrated with the vegetables. This should take 20–30 minutes if you are going to cook the taste of the flour out.

Over a high heat add the stock to this gunge and beat away with a wooden spoon for 5–10 minutes, then pass through a coarse sieve. This is your basic gravy.

Now the fun starts! By adding wine, vinegar, sherry, mustard, tomato purée, horseradish, Worcestershire sauce, mushroom ketchup and so on, you can make the type of gravy to suit your palate. Of course, you don't add *all* these ingredients: to complement turkey I would choose red wine, a little wine vinegar, Worcestershire sauce and perhaps a touch of sherry.

When cold, store the gravy sensibly and re-heat on the day itself.

Vegetables

VEGETABLES CAN OFTEN be where the busy cook falls down, loses composure, begins to wonder if it is all worth the bother and wishes to throw in the towel. Nil desperandum! Just read on.

If you follow my tip, you will get extremely tasty vegetables to go with your turkey but, yes, they will be totally devoid of vitamins and all the other goodies that nutritionists say you should eat. As it's Christmas, you may ignore them this once.

Carrots, parsnips, turnips and Brussels sprouts are the four vegetables you require. It is essential that the carrots and parsnips, when peeled, are cut into circles of even thickness and the turnips into similar-sized chips; also that the sprouts are all about the same size. You can prepare them 2–3 days before, if need be.

Have a large saucepan of boiling water ready, dunk the vegetables into this in a chip basket and, when they come back to the boil, cook for only 2 minutes. Remove at once and run under the cold tap to arrest the cooking.

Prepare four large, well-buttered squares of tinfoil and place one type of vegetable on each. To the carrots add finely chopped preserved ginger, to the parsnips freshly grated nutmeg, to the turnips horseradish cream, and to the sprouts bacon fat saved from breakfasts. Fold each square of foil to resemble a Cornish pasty and, when the vegetables are cold, put in the fridge.

Mid-morning on Christmas Day take them out of the fridge. Put a rack into a roasting tin and place the parcels on this. Pour a little boiling water in the roasting tin and heat the vegetables through for 20 minutes either on on top of the stove, with the water bubbling gently, or in a low oven. This can all be done while the cooked turkey is settling before being carved.

To serve, open the parcels and distribute the vegetables beween the warmed dinner plates. If you are short of space for warming plates, half-fill the sink with hot water and then, one by one, drop the dinner plates on top of each other. (Do this *gently*!) Leave until you wish to use them – about 5 minutes minimum – and then all they need is a quick wipe with a teatowel.

Table setting

*I*F PRACTICAL *and possible, get your main table finished and out of the way the day before. A table setting like mine (see the photo) takes imagination, daring and time, but costs little! I am fortunate in that I can set up the conservatory for the festive feast and then close it off the night before.*

Hanging from the roof I have an angel statue which normally overlooks the staircase. Surrounding this, and secured in a bucket under the table, is a large branch I spotted on one of my autumn walks with my dog, Ozzie. It has been painted with white gloss paint and then hung with Christmas tree balls, bows and cheap storm lanterns holding candles.

This year I have decided to raid my collection of white

cherubs to scatter on the table. The whole setting should be a talking point to break the ice and get the party going. Mind you, I can guess what some guests will say when they leave and turn out of the drive: 'Did you see all that clutter on the table – wasn't it stupid, way over the top as usual.' What miserable people folk like that must be!

The fruit bowl is placed on one of three old glass cake stands. On the other two I put nuts, holly and glass balls.

When you initially lay the table, do set all the glasses you need – but upside-down. It is a relatively easy task to polish them just before your guests come. Simply pour boiling water into a jug, hold the inside of each glass over the steam, and use a clean, soft teatowel to get a superb sparkle.

I put extra candles on the table and round the sides of the room as overall they create a delightful, sparkling effect.

Christmas wines

*F*OR SEVERAL YEARS NOW *I have been slightly disillusioned with many French wines. Take Sancerre, for instance. When I was first introduced to this wine by Margaret Costa, she told me I would always recognise it from its smell of new-mown grass and delicate taste of gooseberries. For years it had both these wonderful qualities. Now practically every supposedly good restaurant in the world sports it, and hardly ever does it taste as I remember. Presumably Sancerre still comes from the same small vineyards in the Loire, so how come production has seemingly quadrupled?*

I find many of the New World wines cleaner, gutsier and positively honest. Get a bottle of Cloudy Bay Sauvignon Blanc from New Zealand and you will immediately know what I meant about the 'old' Sancerre. Nobilo's Chardonnay from their Dixon Estate in New Zealand just shouts of rich, golden, buttery flavours. Also from New Zealand, a Delegats Chardonnay or Sauvignon Blanc are as good as you will find anywhere.

From Australia, my favourite Chardonnays are Hill Smith, Orlando and Pirramimma McLaren Vale, and the Sauvignons are the Cape Mentalle Margaret River and the Cullens.

My favourite Californian wines are those from the Glen Ellen and Clos du Bois houses. And good, basic, party drinking calls for the South African KWV Cape Forêt 1987 and their Roodeberg 1984.

However, on Christmas Day I opened and consumed my two favourite burgundies – the Beaune Clos des Mouches of Joseph Drouhin – the 1983 white and the 1985 red. A sparkling wine which, at the moment, is being slated by the wine experts is the Carlton Brut Pêcher – in other words, a wine tasting of peaches: it does. For a one-off occasion it is lovely and much liked by older folk who go for the sweetness. Try a bottle, do.

Any Uriah Heep or Scrooge, please note with great care that I always have near me a bottle of local Rossendale Valley spring water. This I use for my strong pink gins at Christmas elevenses when I feel the need for a hangover cure – this is a regular heartbeat-starter! But whatever your tipple, I do wish you a very merry Christmas.

Christmas pastries

*T*RADITIONALLY, OF COURSE, *a Christmas pudding should be served on Christmas Day, but I would rather go for a pecan hazelnut pie after the turkey and have the pud itself on Boxing Day, followed by some black bun a week later at New Year. My Nan used to make the latter 2 or 3 weeks before New Year's Eve, and thin wedges were given to everybody who called round to see the New Year in, provided, of course, that they produced a lump of coal in exchange.*

The basic farmhouse pastry recipe is described in great detail on p. 148, but here you want to make three times that recipe — which is slightly different anyway — to have enough for both pecan pie and black bun.

---

18 oz (500 g) self-raising flour

6 oz (175 g) cornflour

18 oz (500 g) softened butter

pinch of salt

6 oz (175 g) caster sugar

3 medium eggs

Make the pastry into a dough as described on p. 149, then divide into three balls and chill. Bring back to room temperature and roll out two of the balls to fit two 9 in (23 cm) loose-bottomed fluted flan tins. Chill these and then bake blind (again, as described on p. 149). Chill the third ball of pastry until you want to use it, then return to room temperature before rolling.

Black bun

Serves 8–12

1 cooked farmhouse pastry base (see left)

chilled farmhouse pastry for the top (see left)

Filling

12 oz (350 g) each of raisins and currants

2 oz (50 g) each of nibbed almonds and crystallised peel

6 oz (175 g) plain flour, sifted

1 teaspoon each of ground cinnamon, ginger and nutmeg

generous pinch of baking powder

2 oz (50 g) soft light brown sugar

3 tablespoons brandy (true Scots would like malt whisky)

4 medium eggs, lightly beaten

Pre-heat the oven to gas mark 4, 350°F (180°C).

For the filling, combine all the dry ingredients in a large mixing bowl and then bring together with the brandy and lightly beaten eggs.

Spread on the base of the cooked flan case, and then roll out the ball of farmhouse pastry to make a lid. Press together to seal as well as you can.

Bake in the pre-heated oven for 1 hour and then cover with tinfoil. Lower the temperature to gas mark 2, 300°F (150°C), and bake for a further hour.

When cold, wrap in tinfoil and store in an air-tight container.

Pecan pie

Serves 8

1 cooked farmhouse pastry base (see left)

Filling

2 oz (50 g) softened butter

2 oz (50 g) caster sugar

4 medium eggs, beaten

4 oz (100 g) ground hazelnuts

finely grated rind of 2 oranges

1 teaspoon ground cinnamon

pinch of ground allspice

1 lb (450 g) golden syrup

6 oz (175 g) whole pecan nuts

Garnish

whipped cream

about 1 oz (25 g) pecan nuts

Pre-heat the oven to gas mark 4, 350°F (180°C).

To make the filling, cream the butter and sugar together, then little by little add the beaten eggs. Fold in the hazelnuts, orange rind, cinnamon, allspice and syrup.

Spread the pecan nuts on the base of the pre-cooked flan and cover with the syrup mix. Bake in the pre-heated oven for 30 minutes, then turn down the temperature to gas mark 2, 300°F (150°C), and cook for a further 20 minutes.

It is very important that you remember to remove the cooked pie from the tin while it is warm as, when cooling, the syrup tends to work through the pastry and can make the sides of the pie stick to the tin. Serve decorated with whipped cream and some extra pecan nuts.

Menu

SAVOURY ONION CUPS

(page 26)

CHICKEN AND LIVER PÂTÉ LOAF

(page 14)

with

POTATO AND MUSHROOM FLAN

(page 104)

LEMON ICE-BOX PUDDING

(page 122)

VEGETABLE TERRINE

(page 34)

WATERCRESS-STUFFED LOIN OF PORK

(page 80)

with

RATATOUILLE

(page 106)

APPLE PIE WITH SAVOURY CHEESE PASTRY

(page 150)

Menu

BAKED RED PEPPER WITH TOMATO

(page 28)

HALIBUT STUFFED WITH GORGONZOLA
AND BAKED IN SPINACH

(page 60)

with
STEAMED VEGETABLES

(page 94)

HOT FRUIT SALAD

(page 116)

MINTED PEA PURÉE HERB SLICE

(page 40)

ROAST RIB OF BEEF WITH MINI-MUSTARD PUDDINGS

(page 70)

with
VEGETABLE CASSEROLE

(page 98)

STICKY TOFFEE PUDDING

(page 134)

with
BUTTERSCOTCH SAUCE

(page 135)

INDEX